INTERNATIONAL SOCIALISM

A quarterly journal of socialist theory

Spring 2002

# Contents

**Issue 94 of INTERNATIONAL SOCIALISM, quarterly journal of the Socialist Workers Party (Britain)**

Published March 2002

Distribution/subscriptions: International Socialism,
PO Box 82, London E3 3LH
E-mail: isj@swp.org.uk
American distribution: B de Boer, 113 East Center Street, Nutley, New Jersey 07110
Editorial and production: 020 7538 5821
Sales and subscriptions: 020 7531 9810

ISBN 1 898876 83 5

Typeset by East End Offset, London E3
Cover design by Sherborne Design
Cover photograph from Popperfoto

A full index for *International Socialism* is available at www.lpi.org.uk

For details of back copies see the end pages of this book

Subscription rates for one year (four issues) are:

| | | |
|---|---|---|
| Britain and overseas (surface): | individual | £14 ($30) |
| | institutional | £25 |
| Air speeded supplement: | North America | £2 |
| | Europe/South America | £2 |
| | elsewhere | £4 |

**Note to contributors**

**The deadline for articles intended for issue 96 of *International Socialism* is 1 June 2002.**

**All contributions should be double spaced with wide margins. Please submit two copies. If you write your contribution using a computer, please also supply a disk, together with details of the computer and program used.**

# INTERNATIONAL SOCIALISM

**A quarterly journal of socialist theory**

**THE PEOPLE** of Argentina exploded onto the streets in December 2001, no longer willing to pay for the crisis caused by their rulers. After toppling four presidents in as many weeks, where will the protests go now? Chris Harman, author of *A People's History of the World*, looks at the history of struggle in Argentina from the pitched battles between workers and the state in 1919 to the present day. He assesses the balance of forces in the current revolt, and asks who is in a position to win the leadership of a struggle whose outcome will be decisive for the global movement against neo-liberalism.

**CLASS STRUGGLE** is back on the agenda as rail workers, post workers, teachers and others are taking to the picket lines in defiance of Blair's privatisation programme. Are we facing a return to the 1970s? As a fourth major union elects a left winger as general secretary, what should our attitude to the trade union bureaucracy be? Martin Smith examines these questions by revisiting the tradition of rank and file organisation.

**ZIMBABWE** has hit the headlines recently, as the British establishment screams about protecting the rights of the whites being forcibly evicted from their land. Mugabe talks of anti-imperialism, but whose side is he really on? What is the situation of the black majority in Zimbabwe? And what is the character of the main opposition party, the Movement for Democratic Change? Leo Zeilig clears up the confusion with his brief history of the Mugabe regime, and his analysis of the current crisis and the left in Zimbabwe.

**PIERRE BOURDIEU**, a leading sociologist and latterly anti-globalisation activist, died in January 2002. Jim Wolfreys remembers the life and work of this important figure on the French left.

**BOOK REVIEWS** include Richard Greeman, executor of Victor Serge's literary estate, on Susan Weissman's *Victor Serge: The Course is Set on Hope*, and Dave Crouch on *The Bolsheviks and the National Question*.

# Argentina: rebellion at the sharp end of the world crisis

CHRIS HARMAN

*There is no resistance to neo-liberalism in Argentina. The left has no impact. There are a few strikes, but they do not raise any challenges to the system.*
**An intervention from the floor by an Argentinian left winger at a 'Globalisation and Resistance' conference in London, February 2001.**

*The television transmitted images of hundreds of demonstrators, mainly women and children, at a supermarket, screaming loudly, 'We want to eat! We want to eat!'... During the day hundreds of supermarkets in the whole country were plundered.*

*The government and media began to speak of 'prevailing anarchy' and of the necessity 'to re-establish order'. President de la Rua informed the population on TV that Wednesday that he had declared a state of siege. People's rights were suspended, any public meeting of more than two people was considered subversive, the mass media could be censored, the repressive machine was free to act and arrest people.*

*As soon as he finished the speech some people began to hit saucepans in their houses. This form of protest (**cacerolazo**) was common at the end of the military dictatorship. Then it extended to the streets to become an organised action. In one hour a million people challenged the state of siege.*

*By midnight the **Plaza de Mayo** square was full, and thousands had substituted the desperate scream of 'We want to eat!' for one more offensive, **'Que se vayan'** ('Get them out!'). They didn't only refer to the government, but to the entire political establishment... They began to chant slogans dedicated to each* *of the main figures of the traditional parties, and even to some union leaders linked to these parties.*

*The police attacked them with horses, sticks, shields, tear gas and rubber bullets. The population's peaceful protest became a true battlefield. Many of those who gathered in* **Plaza de Mayo** *had never participated in a street protest. There were many children and old men.*

*Initially it was easy for the police to corner and frighten the demonstrators. Then the resistance began to be organised. The square was filled with people and so were the steps outside the parliament building. A few hours after the beginning of the protests people knew the finance minister Cavallo had resigned.*

*Then on the Thursday everything began again. By midday people came to the square that had become the battlefield between the people and the government.*

*There were workers on high and low wages, university students in shorts with their T-shirts covering their faces, old ladies with their handbags, street children, office and bank clerks with their shirts and ties, sanitation workers in their uniforms, many indigenous peoples, women with children—all on the same side of the barricades.*

*The repression increased. The police began shooting lead bullets and many people were killed or wounded. The demonstrators answered by attacking McDonald's, the banks, and other symbols of capitalism and the population's poverty. They set on fire several buildings and vehicles. The battle extended to the whole city.*

*At noon the president gave up his post. The government collapsed.*

**Javier Carles, account of events of 19-20 December 2001 in Buenos Aires.**

*When I saw columns coming from all the neighbourhoods of the city after the president announced the state of siege I thought, 'This is like the fall of the wall. This is the fall of the neo-liberal wall.'*

**Protester Ricardo Carcova, 20 December 2001.**

*The social and political crisis in Argentina took the US authorities by surprise. They expected a slow, politically controlled unravelling of debt default. No one had thought seriously of the possibility of political and social chaos.*

*A week after the expected default things do not seem so easy. The US fears the destabilisation can spread to other countries... A veteran American diplomat with experience in the region, comments, 'The Bush administration did not get involved in this crisis because it saw no domestic political benefit in doing so.' Perhaps things will change if it suddenly finds itself facing a political and social crisis spreading across the hemisphere, because then its political opponents will be able to ask, 'Who lost South America?'*

**Carlos Escude in the Buenos Aires paper *La Nacíon*, 3 January, 2002.**

The explosion of anger that erupted onto the streets of Buenos Aires on 19-20 December 2001 did more than pull down a government. It also showed how economic crisis can suddenly create potentially revolutionary situations. In the aftermath, the presidency passed through four different hands until it came to rest in those of Duhalde, vice-president in the late 1980s and afterwards governor of Buenos Aires. The turmoil in the streets shows no signs of diminishing as I write six weeks later. There are reports of *cacerolazo* protests in Buenos Aires itself and similar protests in scores of provincial towns. Following the accounts on, for instance, the website of the *Azul* television channel is rather like reading descriptions of Germany in 1923, the year of an aborted revolutionary rising and the failed Nazi beerhall *putsch*. In place after place unemployed pickets have been blocking roads, hungry people have been invading supermarkets to demand food, and people whose bank accounts have been frozen have been attacking banks. The leader of the governing party in the Senate has talked openly of the possibility of 'civil war'. The government has suspended repayment of its foreign debts, launched vitriolic denunciations of the owners of privatised concerns, and even sent police to inspect the books of foreign-owned banks. Yet at the same time it is trying to reassure the IMF that it will come to some arrangement to restore capitalist normality and is reassuring foreign-owned banks that it is not out to harm them.

Few observers believe that the government can assuage the discontent that is raging within the middle class and the working class alike, or that it can satisfy the demands of international capitalism. Like any government in the midst of near-revolutionary upheaval, it is pulled in one direction, then in the other and back again, unable to maintain any continuity of policy, unable to think about much except its own survival.

It is still too early to see clearly how things are going to develop. Some commentators have spoken of the 'collapse of the state'. That is an overstatement. The state's bodies of armed men were able to kill at least 24 protesters in Buenos Aires on 20 December, and another 20 in other towns. They have continued to attack protests since, especially in the provinces. But that there has been an enormous weakening of the authority of the state there can be no doubt. And the armed forces, so often in the past the arbiters of the country's politics, have to date been unwilling to intervene. One officer told reporters, 'Even if the situation turns to anarchy or to civil war, if they ask me to intervene my principal concern will be making sure my orders will be obeyed by my men'.[1]

Such a condition of instability cannot last forever. The disparate elements within the Argentinian ruling class are trying desperately to work out some common strategy for regaining control of events and bringing to an end the insurgency in the streets. If they are successful, there is no doubt that they will then use all the forces of the state to reimpose their version of 'order' and wreak vengeance on those who have challenged their power. But they are still a long way from being able to do this. Meanwhile, the Argentinian upheaval has enormous significance for the global system and for the opposition to it that has emerged worldwide in the two and a half years since the Seattle anti-capitalist demonstration.

**Argentinian precedents**

As in any great popular rebellion, people in Argentina have been reaching back in their collective memories for precedents. Three times in the 20th century huge upsurges from below have led to clashes with the state, resulting in outcomes that had a profound effect on social development for years afterwards.

The first such great clash was in January 1919—that year of worldwide revolutionary upheaval. The *Semana Trágica* (Tragic Week) saw bloody battles between workers and the forces of the state in Buenos Aires. The police launched a fierce attack on the Vasena metallurgical plant workers, who had been on strike for several days. Some 200,000 workers, led by anarchist union leaders, marched on the plant. A fierce gun battle broke out, but the police were overwhelmed by the workers. The government then ordered the army to march on the city, and other, syndicalist-led, unions responded by calling a general strike, which was highly effective at first. But eventually the sheer level of repression began to have an effect. Individual unions broke ranks as groups of right wing civilians joined with the police and the army in launching attacks against the working class districts, raiding union buildings and murdering workers. According to the socialist press the final toll was 700 dead and 4,000 injured. The following year the military broke syndicalist-led strikes of farm workers in Patagonia, executing 1,500 strikers.

The outcome of these struggles was decisive in influencing the pattern of Argentinian politics over the next two decades: 'There was a general weakening of the unions in the 1920s, while the role of the army as a key arbiter in national politics was enhanced'.[2] It was able, after a coup in 1930, to bring in a 'decade of infamy', during which conservative governments ruled the country through electoral fraud, corruption and the virtual exclusion of the workers from political life.[3]

The next great confrontation was that of 17 October 1945, 'an event which has passed into the mythology of the Argentinian labour movement. On that day the working class entered the political scene in a massive and explosive manner'.[4]

In 1943 a group of nationalist minded officers had seized power. They did so at a time when economic expansion was leading to a renewed spread of working class militancy and one of them, Juan Peron, took it on himself to try to control this. He did so by insisting employers concede to certain of the demands of workers. This enabled leaders who backed his political ambitions to win the support they needed to dominate the major unions, which grew rapidly in size and influence. By 1945 major sections of the ruling class felt he had gone too far. They persuaded his fellow officers to remove him from the government.

Workers saw this attack on a colonel who had made concessions to them as a threat to their living standards and their dignity. As a wave of strikes spread across the country, the CGT union federation called for a general strike. Huge columns of workers marched on the *Plaza de Mayo* in the centre of Buenos Aires, frightening the military and forcing them to reinstate Peron. The momentum of the victory on the streets ensured that he won a clear majority in presidential elections the following year and ruled the country until 1955.

The workers' victory was double edged. It created circumstances which forced employers to increase real wages by more than 30 percent over the next four years. The union leaders exercised significant influence in the Justicialist Party set up by Peron. His government introduced a version of the welfare state, with union recognition, paid holidays, compensation for redundancy and welfare benefits. But the form the victory took also tied workers and the labour movement to the Peronist myth, with a cult following for his wife 'Evita'—and to a nationalism which preached the unity of 'patriotic' employers and workers, holding that 'international capitalism is an instrument of exploitation, national capital an instrument of welfare'.[5]

The third great upsurge was the *Cordobazo* of 1969—the Argentinian equivalent of the French May and the Italian 'Hot Autumn'. It took place against the background of two decades of attacks on real wages and working conditions.

A decline in real wages had begun under Peron, but the unions were still too strong for the liking of Argentinian capitalism. In 1955 the military overthrew Peron. There was not the immediate, co-ordinated workers' revolt of ten years earlier. But massive repression was needed to beat back widespread resistance, with pitched street battles, a two-day general strike and armed sabotage. In the following decade Argentinian capitalism seized every opportunity to victimise militants, impose speed-ups, 'rationalise' industry and cut back real wages. Every success of workers in resisting attacks on their living standards was followed by escalating inflation, enabling the employers to restore their profits, and then recessions that sapped the will of workers to fight back in the face of state repression. By 1960 real wages in Buenos Aires were back to their level of 1947,[6] and by 1965 the workers' share of national output had fallen from 49.9 percent to 40.7 percent.[7] This was the other side of the 'developmentist' strategy of a ruling class which wanted the profits to enable it to build up heavy industries capable of competing on world markets.

Such attacks created deepening bitterness within the working class. It found expression in enormous loyalty to the Peronist trade union bureaucracy and in a political identification with the exiled Peron so great that he would have won any genuinely open and free election. This caused the military intervention against civilian governments in 1962 and 1966 followed by the military dictatorship of General Onganía. The dictatorship froze wages, smashed strikes and took over unions that put up resistance. It also banned all political parties, including those of the bourgeoisie, and tried to impose military control at every level of society—for instance, taking control of the universities.

The armed forces killed two students during demonstrations against meal prices in May 1969. Protest demonstrations and local strikes erupted and the union federations called a national general strike for 30 May.[8]

Córdoba was the centre of a motor industry that had only emerged in the previous 20 years. Pay was better than in many other industries, and some saw its workers as 'labour aristocrats'. But the newness of the industry and the relative youth of its workforce meant they were less weighed down by the experience of previous defeats and less subordinate to the national union bureaucracies. The car and power plants decided to supplement the general strike with an 'active strike' on 29 May. Columns of workers—some armed with Molotov cocktails—marched on the city centre, the location of the police HQ, the hotels and the banks. There were '4,000 IKA-Renault workers, 10,000 metallurgical workers, 1,000 power workers, and so on'.[9] The workers eventually put to flight 4,000 police and took control of the city centre. Some 5,000 fully armed soldiers then joined battle, forcing the workers to retreat to the working class and student districts, where they threw up barricades. The repression that followed killed 16 people, but did not stop the uprising exposing the vulnerability of the military government and the power of mass mobilisations. It opened up a three-year period of massive strikes, factory occupations, the holding of managers as hostages, violent demonstrations, guerrilla attacks on the forces of the state, and another violent rising in Córdoba, the *Viborazo*.[10]

This wave of struggles did not finally subside until after the military, on behalf of the ruling class as a whole, had permitted the return of Peron to the country. He assumed the presidency in October 1973. The governments run by him and, after his death in June 1974, his third wife Isabel, played very much the same role as that of the governments which oversaw the

'Social Contract' in Britain, the 'Pact of Moncloa' in Spain and the 'historic compromise' in Italy. The Perons were able to use their influence over the trade union bureaucracies to regain a degree of control over working class militancy through a *Pacto Social*, while the bourgeoisie and its state regrouped their forces. But the regrouping took a much bloodier form in Argentina than in Western Europe. Far right groups began to be given a free hand to physically liquidate their opponents. On the very day of Peron's return to the country right wing paramilitaries attacked left wingers among the crowd of 2 million that greeted him at the airport, killing a large number. During the three years of Peronist government scores of left wingers and rank and file union activists were murdered, while the union leaders collaborated with the government. Then in 1976 the military overthrew Isabel Peron and launched the bloodiest assault any working class movement anywhere in the world had suffered since the Second World War, murdering 30,000 left wingers and rank and file activists.

## The character of the struggle in Argentina

The three great popular eruptions of the 20th century had one central thing in common. They were clashes between the industrial working class on the one hand and the bourgeoisie and its state on the other. They were class confrontations that grew out of the internal dynamics of the development of Argentinian capitalism, not from some other mode of production or some extraneous factor. This is important, because the language used to describe Argentina often conceals this reality—and conceals the roots of the eruption on 19-20 December.

Argentina is usually categorised by mainstream economists as an 'emerging market' or a 'developing economy'. The implication is that it is moving from being a poor agricultural country towards being an advanced industrial country, and any problems it faces are because it is not moving fast enough. Some on the left use their own version of the same idea, speaking of a 'dependent' economy, a 'Third World country' or 'a semi-colony'.[11]

There is acute poverty in the country today, and it has long existed in the vast but sparsely populated rural areas and in the shanty towns around cities like Buenos Aires and Córdoba. But this is not because Argentina was historically a 'poor agricultural' country of the 'Third World'. A century ago it was a country with an economy very similar to that of Australia, Canada or New Zealand, devoted to the export of highly profitable products of large scale capitalist agriculture (meat, wool, grain) to Western Europe and was widely called 'the granary of the world'. Its workforce were not Third World indigenous peoples (most of these had been exterminated, US-style, in the 19th century), but immigrants and seasonal workers from Spain and

Italy attracted by wages that were higher than in southern Europe. Output per worker was considerably higher than in France and Italy.[12] Its ruling class had close links with that of Britain—the country was a prime venue for upper class British emigrants, there was a lot of British capital, and about a third of exports went to Britain—but was independent enough to levy protectionist tariffs against British industrial imports and to stay neutral during the First World War (while every British colony and dominion contributed money and men to the imperialist war effort).[13] 'Argentina, at the start of World War One, had reached being a modern capitalist state,' says a Marxist history of Peronism.[14]

The problem for the different sections of its capitalist class throughout the 20th century was not that Argentina lacked national political independence. It had enjoyed this since 1816. The problem was that the Argentinian ruling class controlled a state with a relatively small domestic market and relatively few resources in a world of much wealthier capitalist classes with bigger markets and far greater resources. The message was brought home to them with a vengeance whenever the world price of agricultural goods fell, and with it their profits. This happened with the great slump of the inter-war years, when the world price of wheat fell by 75 percent. 'The Argentinian bourgeoisie, which believed itself to be part of the world's powerful elite, discovered the fragility of the equilibrium on which its wealth rested... It could use force to adjust its boundaries with Chile or Bolivia, but it could not force the French to open their country to its grain or meat'.[15]

Its response, from the 1930s onwards, was to try to redirect agricultural profits into the building up of supposedly less vulnerable manufacturing and extractive industries catering for a very heavily protected domestic market. Governments dominated by the agrarian capitalist interests (often referred to as the 'oligarchy') began this process, Peron intensified it in the late 1940s, and the post-Peronist governments of the 1950s and 1960s continued along the same path. The industrial capitalist class, now overshadowing the old agrarian capitalist oligarchy, was made up of two interlinked groupings. A mass of private capitalists presided over small and medium industry, while state bureaucrats (including military officers) ran most of the new, large scale industries like iron and steel, autos, power generation and oil. Each maintained certain connections with the trade union bureaucracies, who were thus enmeshed in a web of corruption.

Such measures enabled Argentina to industrialise. Only 13 percent of the population worked on the land as against 34 percent in industry in the early 1970s.[16] The rate of industrial expansion in these years was comparable to that in Italy (then referred to by mainstream economists as undergoing a 'miracle', although still one of the poorer West European countries).[17] Some figures for 1972 illustrate the smallness of the distance separating Argentina and Italy at that time:[18]

| | *Argentina* | *Italy* |
|---|---|---|
| *Kilograms of meat per person per year* | 90 | 47 |
| *Litres of milk per person per year* | 70 | 65 |
| *Litres of seed oil per person per year* | 10.3 | 7.9 |
| *Calories per person per day* | 3,170 | 2,940 |
| *Cars per 100 people* | 11.6 | 20.9 |
| *TVs per 100 people* | 14.9 | 18.9 |
| *Newspapers per 1,000 people* | 128 | 85 |
| *Inhabitants per dwelling* | 3.8 | 3.1 |
| *University students per 1,000 people* | 11.4 | 11.7 |
| *Doctors per 1,000 people* | 18.9 | 18.0 |
| *Mortality rate per 1,000 people* | 8.8 | 9.6 |
| *Life expectancy* | 67.06 | 65.77 |

There were differences between the two countries—Argentinians did slightly better as regards foodstuffs, Italians as regards consumer durables. But they were differences between countries at comparable levels of 'development', quite unlike those which would appear if the comparison were, say, between Italy and India, or for that matter between Argentina and Guatemala. And Argentina was probably less dependent on foreign capital and foreign imports. Imports only accounted for 1 percent of Argentinian consumer products, and foreign capital, although important in certain industries, accounted for only 5 percent of total fixed investment (as against 15.4 percent in 1943).[19]

There has been an enormous change since 1972. A wide gap has opened up between the living standards of the mass of people in the two countries. With an average hourly manufacturing wage of only $1.67 an hour even before the present slump—and with very large numbers of people getting less—Argentina today is experiencing levels of poverty not known in Italy since the 1940s.[20] Even the average calorific intake has fallen (although it was still at a similar level to Britain in the mid-1990s, and a third higher than in countries like Guatemala and Bolivia).[21] This is not, however, because of 'underdevelopment' in Argentina. Rather it is because of the contradictions facing a weak capitalism once it has reached a certain stage of development. From a capitalist point of view Argentina has 'developed' since 1972—yet the condition of the majority of its population has got worse.

No national capitalist ruling class can ever rest on its laurels. Rival national capitalisms are accumulating endlessly, and it cannot afford to lag behind. One ruling over a relatively small economy finds the problems particularly acute, even if the economy is industrial rather than agrarian. Ensuring protected domestic markets has in the past provided a short term solution to some of these problems. But the narrowness of the market means costs of production are likely to be disproportionately high, and the resources at hand for further accumulation correspondingly limited. Hence continual efforts to raise the rate of exploitation as much as possible and repeated restructuring to forcibly shift capital from the hands of small business to those of big business. This is what Argentinian capitalism has been doing for more than half a century. It explains the ferocity of its confrontations with the working class, its political instability, the recurrent resorts to military rule and, most recently, the opening up of the economy to the multinationals, international finance and the dictates of the International Monetary Fund.

Argentina's capitalists had been able to hide from this problem to some extent during the first five years of Peron's rule. Food shortages in post-war Europe doubled the price to be obtained for Argentina's agricultural exports, and the high profits that flowed back to the country enabled the government to buy off working class discontent and industrialise to the benefit of the middle and small bourgeoisie at the same time. By the same token, however, the collapse of agricultural prices in the early 1950s pulled the rug from under Peron's methods. From 1951 onwards Argentinian capitalism could only continue building up industry by increasing the rate of exploitation. This meant cutting into the living standards workers had come to enjoy. And to keep Argentinian capitalism abreast of its rivals in the world system, accumulation had to be increasingly in industries producing means of production rather than those that could provide the consumer goods workers and the middle classes wanted. For capitalist industry to grow, living standards had to fall.

This explains why the ruling class sent Peron into exile in 1955—and why those sections of Peronism who were tied by various strings to the national capitalists were unwilling to put up serious opposition to his overthrow. It also explains why the period 1955 to 1983 saw brief periods of rule by civilian elected governments interspersed with longer or shorter periods of military dictatorship. Every spell of industrial expansion drew new people into the workplaces and increased the feeling of working class confidence, which found expression both in industrial militancy and in support for 'populist' Peronist politicians who promised at least a partial return to the living standards and welfare provisions people had known in the past. Civilian governments were unable to resist such pressures for long. But Argentinian capitalism definitely did want to resist them, and eventually opted for the return of the hard men from the military to restore order.

The final such cycle was that which ran from the *Cordobazo*, through the Peronist governments of the 1970s, to the military dictatorship of the junta. The new Peronist governments tried to buy off working class discontent without cutting unduly into industrial profits by printing money, so that prices were rising by 20 or 30 percent a month in mid-1975. The 'restoration of order' by the military dictatorship in 1976 was much more vicious than any before. It was not just a matter of the mass killings. There was also an unprecedented attack on workers' living standards. Real wages in 1978 were only about half what they had been in 1975.[22] This meant they were at a lower level than in 1940.[23]

The attacks on workers and the left were accompanied by a massive rationalisation of industry brought about by an over-valuation of the peso which turned the country into a paradise for speculators. The manufacturing workforce was cut by about a fifth in four years, while productivity from the remaining workers was forced up by 37 percent.[24] Meanwhile half a million workers in the public sector lost their jobs. Yet these measures were not enough to overcome the intrinsic problems of Argentinian capitalism. Economic growth in 1979 was followed by stagnation in 1980 and recession in 1981, while annual inflation remained at over 100 percent. There was growing discontent not only from the impoverished working class, but also from sections of Argentinian capitalism. The war over the Malvinas/Falkland Islands was an attempt to divert attention from these problems. Its failure spelt the end of the dictatorship in 1983. But not the end of the problems of Argentinian capitalism.

## A capitalist class in search of a strategy

The victory of the Radical Party of Alfonsin in the presidential elections of 1983 opened the way for a rerun of the classic pattern of civilian governments. Workers pushed to restore the loss in living standards they had suffered under the junta. Argentinian capitalism was not strong enough to deliver these and raised prices to recoup its profits. There were a couple of years of rising output. Then inflation reached astronomic levels—1,470 percent in the 12 months up to June 1989, 20,226 percent in the 12 months up to March 1990—just as the economy went into a deep slump.[25] Meanwhile the level of foreign debt had doubled to about $60 billion. Workers suffered economically even more than under the junta—real wages in 1989 were about 25 percent below the already desperate 1980 level. There was a sense of immense crisis for both the capitalists and the working class.

The unions organised no fewer than 14 general strikes in this period. Real hunger now stalked a working population which had once been among the best fed in the world, and there were food riots with the looting of supermarkets in Buenos Aires in 1989. But the old outcome of crises and disillusionment with an elected government, the military coup, could no longer work—three attempted coups in 1987-1988 all collapsed in the face of massive popular opposition (a million people took to the streets against the first) and splits within the armed forces. Instead there was an electoral change, with the routing of Alfonsin's Radical Party by the Peronist Menem in the presidential elections of 1989.

The crisis of the Alfonsin government drove home to Argentinian capitalists the desperate need to find a new economic strategy. Despite its repeated drives to accumulate and its desperate desire to be competitive internationally, output per head was actually a fifth lower than ten years before.[26] The most powerful and advanced sections of capital had long before begun to press for a new strategy:

> *The Onganía dictatorship (of 1966-70) already responded to the need for Argentinian capitalism to prepare the conditions of a new scheme of accumulation based on a rupture with the autarky and the entry of industry into world markets. Expanded accumulation needed to pass from the development of an internal market protected by the state through customs barriers to the savage struggle to create space between the great powers of the world market.*[27]

The shift from the old strategy was slowed down by the political pressures that arose with the upturn of working class struggle in the late 1960s and early 1970s. It was only with the coming to power of the military junta in 1976 that big capital felt free to push its new 'neo-liberal' approach. Reduced tariffs and a high exchange rate led to a flood of imports which undercut a lot of the old medium and small scale firms, and the total number of person hours worked in manufacturing industry fell by 20 percent.

Sections of the regime continued, however, to use the power of the state to try to foster certain industries which were run by the monopolies and sections of the state—'machinery and equipment', iron and steel, infrastructure development, electricity and gas, arms production and agriculture all expanded from 1976 to 1980.[28] The military-run state saw the revenues to be obtained from exports of food—now mainly to the USSR—as a source for building up national industrial power (and buying arms). So the state was responsible for more than half of total investment in the years 1976-1978.[29] Big capital grew at the expense of small capital as well as through increased exploitation of the working class. But it still lacked the competitiveness it sought in international markets. Free market perfectionists blamed this on the remaining state controls and nationalised industries.

The crisis of the late 1980s provided them with the political opportunity they wanted to dump these things. The desperate plight in which people found themselves reduced the likelihood of either the working class or the middle bourgeoisie putting up resistance. As living standards sank through the floor and inflation reached unbelievable heights, every class was desperate for an alternative of some sort.

Menem came to office promising to provide this. He had enormous backing from the trade union bureaucracy and most workers. But he also had connections with sections of big business desperate for the new model of accumulation, and turned to the former head of the national bank under the dictatorship, the Harvard trained economist, Domingo Cavallo, to provide it. Cavallo held the messianic view that neo-liberalism was the answer to the problems of Argentinian capitalism.

## The neo-liberal miracle maker

> *It's springtime in Buenos Aires. The government is selling everything in sight. Huge billboards announce auctions of office buildings on the chic Calle Florida and waterfront acreage down by the docks. Army regiments are being booted out of Buenos Aires so that prime real estate can go on the block. Even the giraffes, ostriches and a 48 year old Indian elephant named Norma now have a private owner, after the city fathers sold the zoo.*
>
> *The privatisation process stretches far beyond the city. For the first time ever, the government is opening oil fields to private investors. The cash infusion is ending the decade-old debt crisis. 'In a few months, it will be ancient history,' boasts Domingo Cavallo, Argentina's economic minister. As a result, investors are now flocking to Latin America.*
>
> *The change in the past three years amounts to nothing less than economic revolution. At the centre of it is privatisation. While Communism collapsed noisily in Europe, Latin America's old orthodoxy, centering on state-run strategic industries, crumbled quietly. Now, the Latins, like the Eastern Europeans, are bowing to the private market and racing for investments to revive their bedraggled economies. The change means megabusiness for First World bankers, who are introducing a continent to the financing and merger and acquisition tricks from up North—and collecting hefty commissions for the help.*

So gushed *Business Week* in 1991.[30] Its optimism not only about the profits to be got from Argentina, but also about the ending of the old cycle of crises and indebtedness, was shared by most of the world's business media and economic 'experts'. There was still enormous enthusiasm six years later, despite a brief recession hitting Argentina after the Mexican 'Tequila' crisis of 1994. 'I am very optimistic,' said Mr Walter Molano, director of economic and financial research at SBC Warburg in New York.

'The country is clearly seeing the payoff from the reforms undertaken in 1991-1995, some of which have a long gestation period.' Growth the next year should have a floor of 6 percent, he added.[31] The *Financial Times* extolled 'the resilience of the economy after the reforms'.[32]

The 'reforms' amounted to a massive implementation of the measures embodied in the 'Washington Consensus' as preached by the IMF and the World Bank—privatisation of virtually all government-owned industries and services, the replacement of state pensions and health benefits by private schemes, the slashing of remaining tariffs on imports, the encouraging of foreign capital inflows, and, to cap all these other measures, a rigid fixing of the peso's value to that of the US dollar (known as 'the dollar peg') in 1992. In return for this package of measures the IMF agreed to help the Argentinian government renegotiate its debt payments as part of the overall Brady Plan for Latin America.

The assumption behind this package of measures was that they would further push the restructuring of industry, 'shaking out' people from the public sector and inefficient private firms, while encouraging an inflow of foreign capital that would modernise Argentinian industry and enable it, at last, to compete internationally. This fitted in with Argentina establishing the Mercosur regional common market with Brazil, Uruguay and Paraguay.

Such measures were obviously met with joy in international financial circles who were set to gain from buying up Argentinian businesses on the cheap. They were just as welcome to key sections of Argentina's ruling class, who could move from being big fish in the small Argentinian pond to being medium fish in a world sized lake. But, for a time at least, very large numbers of the lower middle class and workers also acquiesced to them, such was the desperation to escape from the crisis at the turn of the decade and such were the illusions in Menem as a Peronist 'friend of the workers'.

The reforms were accompanied at first by some limited improvement in the conditions of large numbers of people as the economy grew through to 1994. Average real wages stopped falling and rose above their 1989 low point.[33] And for a couple of years there was a growth in employment in most sectors.[34] The self employed and the small business sectors of the middle class felt that the threat of immediate bankruptcy had gone. The salaried sections of the middle class (or, more accurately speaking, the better off sections of the white collar working class) saw their differentials as against semi-skilled and unskilled workers' increase.[35] The sense, at least for some people, that things might be beginning to get better, was sufficient for Menem to win the presidential election of 1994 and his Peronist party the mid-term congressional elections of 1996. As with the 'Thatcher-Lawson' boom of Britain in the late 1980s, there was just enough movement in the conditions of a considerable number of people to make the illusion of permanent change and talk of a 'miracle' stick.

But by 1992 rationalisation and restructuring of industry were occurring in earnest. There was a massive destruction of certain jobs—about one in ten jobs in manufacturing and about one in five in electricity, water and gas. Unemployment began to climb sharply, reaching 18 percent in 1994-1995. And from then on high unemployment persisted despite renewed recovery from 1995 to 1998. While extolling the effect of 'reform' in 1997, the *Financial Times* was able to note:

> *Higher growth has failed to translate into a significant fall in the unemployment rate, despite signs that job creation is rising. The high level of joblessness was one factor behind an increase in social tensions during the year.*[36]

So for the mass of workers, the 'miracle' meant only that real wages remained more or less static at their historically low level, while a growing pool of people were faced with long term unemployment. Since unemployment compensation lasts for a few months only, this translated into growing pools of deep poverty.

But the 'miracle' hardly matched up to the historic hopes of the Argentinian bourgeoisie either. Gross National Output grew by about 25 percent. But this only put it back roughly where it had been ten years before. And the industries Argentinian capitalism had sought to create over the previous half century were not able to conquer world markets—or even the regional market formed by Mercosur. Instead, as under the junta, foreign goods flooded into the country while exports remained subdued. There were recurrent balance of payments deficits.

Infusions of foreign capital and the privatisation receipts were able to hide the gap and conceal essential weaknesses, allowing Cavallo each year to assure fellow members of the ruling class that a dramatic breakthrough was about to occur. What he chose to forget was that foreign capital that could flow into a country at great speed could flow out again even more quickly the moment any event shook its confidence in the level of profits to be obtained. Meanwhile levels of foreign debt crept inexorably higher.

## The crash and the crunch

The moment of truth came with the impact on Latin America of the Asian crisis of 1997. Suddenly, financiers and business people everywhere were shocked into worrying about their investments in supposedly safe and profitable 'emerging markets'—including those of Latin America—and moved their money out of them. Argentina was pushed back into recession, only two years after recovering from the recession associated with the Mexican crisis of 1994. And the loans the government and businesses depended on were increasingly costly as lenders, foreign and Argentinian alike, demanded massive premiums over and above normal interest rates. As Joseph Stiglitz, the mainstream economist who was sacked for being critical of the World Bank, has pointed out:

> *East Asia's crisis of 1997 became a global financial crisis, raising interest rates for all emerging markets, including Argentina. Argentina's exchange system survived, but at a heavy price—double digit unemployment. Soon high interest rates strained the country's budget...With 20 percent interest rates, 9 percent of the country's GDP was spent annually on financing its debt. The US dollar, to which Argentinian's peso was tied, increased sharply in value. Meanwhile, Argentina's Mercosur trading partner, Brazil, saw its currency depreciate. Wages and prices fell, but not enough to allow Argentina to compete effectively.*[37]

Argentinian capitalism's longstanding weakness when it came to competing with Brazil was exacerbated as Brazil's devaluation made its goods cheaper, both on international markets and inside Argentina. Argentinian companies, unable to borrow easily, set out to protect their profits by cutting down production lines and cutting wages. Car production sagged 47 percent in a year.[38] The number employed in textiles and footwear was half what it was in 1990.[39] And then, last year, the economic crisis beginning in the three centres of advanced world capitalism (the US, the European Union and Japan) began to bite. Unemployment soared upwards until it reached 20 percent and private sector wages were slashed by a fifth from their already low levels.

The sackings and wage slashing exacerbated the crisis of the small and medium business sectors. By September 2001 total sales of goods were down 8.4 percent on the previous year and sales through 'shopping malls' down 21 percent.[40] Official figures were by now showing that 40 percent of the population were living below the poverty line. This was an economic catastrophe comparable to that which hit countries like Germany and the United States in the early 1930s.

But things got even worse in the last quarter of the year. The country was running a trade deficit and the government was spending more than its income, since each contraction of the economy reduced tax revenues (they fell 14 percent in the year to September 2001). It simply did not have enough dollars to continue paying its bills—and its whole political approach ruled out seizing these dollars from the Argentinian rich, who were moving their own money to safe havens abroad. It could only keep going by turning to the International Monetary Fund, which demanded further cuts in government spending.

This meant pursuing an economic policy mainstream economists used to insist had been the fatal 'mistake' of the 1930s which would never be adopted again. Every cut in government spending was bound to deepen the recession, and every deepening of the recession was bound to make the government deficit greater by cutting its revenues further. Nevertheless, this is what the IMF recommended—and what Argentinian governments of both the main capitalist parties accepted.

## The politics of recession

The onset of renewed recession had doomed the Menem government. The 1999 election resulted in a clear victory for an alliance of the Radical Party and a new, supposedly left wing, electoral bloc—Frepaso. But the new government proceeded to follow the same policies as its predecessor, introducing a cuts package in May 2000 and then again a year later. Popular resistance forced the president, de la Rua, to withdraw the March 2001 package and to sack its author, Lopéz Murphy. But the supporters of neoliberalism were soon ecstatic, for de la Rua replaced him with Cavallo. The return of the 'miracle workers', they said, could once again dig Argentinian capitalism out of its hole.

Within five months his miracle working power proved to be fraudulent. He was forced to turn to the IMF for more funds, agreeing to still more drastic budget cuts and imposing 13 percent reductions in public sector wages and pensions—with the blessing of Tony Blair who stopped off in Argentina before going on to holiday in Mexico. By this time, however, it was becoming clear that whatever he did, apart from imposing mass starvation on the country, there was no way Cavallo could balance the government's budget. As a *Financial Times* editorial had to admit:

> *It is now clear that Argentina is unable to escape its slow motion train wreck by orthodox means. Because output is falling, the fiscal position is worsening. That impairs confidence, which has pushed interest rates on dollar borrowing to almost 20 percentage points above those on US treasuries. With such interest rates, the economy can only implode. The logical step then seems to be a combination of devaluation with default. But the fear has been that this would merely trigger a flight from the currency and a return to very high inflation. Moreover, if substantial dollar liabilities remained, there could still be mass bankruptcy.*[41]

A week later a former chief economist of the IMF stated the heretical view that there was no way the government could clear the deficits as the IMF wanted:

> *Realistic appraisal of Argentina's plight carries...implications for international policy making. This year's public sector deficit will be much greater than the IMF programme target of about $6 billion... This year's fiscal deficit will probably run to between $20 billion and $25 billion. With the economy deeply mired in recession, the government's true financing requirements for 2002 probably cannot be reduced below $12 billion to $15 billion.*[42]

Cavallo was not prepared to listen to such talk. He even resisted suggestions from some in the IMF that he should follow the Brazilian example and devalue the peso. Meanwhile, the IMF itself was refusing to do anything positive to help him out. The Republican administration in Washington did not regard Argentina as strategically important and was talking about the 'moral hazard' of easing Argentina's debt burden. It even went so far as to suggest that those who had been foolhardy enough to lend money to the country should accept some of the burden of their mistake. No doubt this view was encouraged by the fact that European—especially Spanish—companies would be disproportionately more damaged by an Argentinian collapse than US ones.[43] And so the IMF began making it clear that it would not release funds it had promised Cavallo unless there were further savage cuts. Already, provincial governments, unable to pay their workers with proper currency, were resorting to the use of special coupons, supposedly exchangeable for goods in certain shops.

Now Cavallo turned to measures that impoverished not only the workers but a vast sector of Argentina's self employed and professional middle class. He took money from the privatised pension funds to pay interest owed on the debt, and then imposed the fencing off (*corralito*) of all personal bank accounts, so that people could not withdraw more than $1,000 a month (around £150 a week). People rushed to try to get money out of their accounts—and found themselves faced with empty cash machines and endless queues. Then, on 17 December, he introduced a new $9 billion cuts package.

Much of the media internationally presented the *corralito* as only hitting the well to do. In fact, the very well do to had long before moved their dollars to safer havens abroad. The *corralito* did hit the middle and lower sections of the traditional petty bourgeoisie—self employed professionals, small business people with a couple of employees, shopkeepers. These groups would keep most of their income in the banks and would look to their savings to see them through rough patches due to lack of business, illness or failure of other people to pay their bills to them. They could now suddenly be left with no income. So too could vast numbers of white collar workers whose salaries had been paid straight into their bank accounts. Finally, many of the manual unemployed also relied on the banks to stay alive, after putting any redundancy payment or past savings into them.

In reality, what Cavallo was doing with the *corralito* was declaring that Argentinian capitalism and its state cared no more for the so called middle classes than for the workers. It was the ultimate act of proletarianisation. The impoverished middle classes responded by swarming onto the streets with the unemployed on 19-20 December—and driving the government from office.

### *Cacerolazos* and *piqueteros*

The uprising of 19-20 December was 'spontaneous' in the sense that no single body issued a call for it and no single political force directed its development. It was reminiscent of 14 July 1789 and February 1848 in France, February 1917 in Russia, November 1918 in Germany, October 1956 in Hungary, May 1968 in France—and, more recently, December 1989 in Romania, 1997 in Albania, and 2000 in Serbia. On each occasion, the anger of myriad different groups with their own particular grievances suddenly fused into an explosive force which established rulers could not resist. Some of the rulers ran for their lives. Others bowed before the force of the angry movement in order to try to re-establish their full control at a later date.

Accounts of the Argentinian uprising tell how it had various sources. There were the hungry people who gathered outside supermarkets demanding food and who turned to looting and to attacking banks when they did not get it. There were the people who began gathering in the districts (*barrios*), banging their cooking pots (*cacerolas*) in anger at the *corralito*, and then moving towards the city centre. There were the young people who flooded to join the mobilisation once it was under way. There were the *Madres de la Plaza de Mayo*—women protesting, as they did every Thursday, against the 'disappearance' of their children and husbands during the junta's dirty war. But once these groups had come together, fighting back despite the police killing 23 people in Buenos Aires (and another 20 nationally), so as to force Cavallo to resign and President de la Rua to flee, there was the sense of movement to the *cacerolazo* ('cooking pot event') that transcended their particular demands. So it was that nine days later they were on the streets again, this time directing their anger against Cavallo's successor, Rodriguez Saá, and invading the Congress to force his resignation. And three weeks later, the Buenos Aires mainstream newspaper *Página 12* could describe a further wave of protests as, 'The spectre which puts fear into the Pink House [presidential palace]'.[44]

By this time there was a certain set pattern to the protests in Buenos Aires. So *Página 12* describes a typical protest involving both well-to-do middle class and poorer districts:

> *The* ***cacerolazo*** *began in many points in the city and was growing in numbers and intensity. In the* ***Barrio Norte*** *they started on the balconies and in the doorways, with cars sounding the horns enthusiastically. There were still no songs or banners, and no one had blocked the road, but the volume of sound began to deafen you. By 9pm in the* ***Belgrano*** *neighbourhood they began to come down from the buildings into the street. There was a group banging metal and singing... Another group began to grow in* ***Cabildo*** *and* ***Juramento****. In* ***San Cristóbal****, a neighbourhood very active in the previous* ***cacerolazos****, people gathered in* ***San Juan*** *and* ***La Rioja****. At 1pm the concentration in front of the congress began. First a few dozen, then some hundreds and finally ever larger groups arrived from other neighborhoods along roads which were completely blocked. When there was a critical mass, a column formed up which began to go down towards the* ***Plaza de Mayo****.*[45]

The aim of the protesters was to bring about a change in government policy—or even a change in government as they had on 20 and 29 December. And when they were not immediately successful, the younger and poorer sections of the crowd would attempt to fight their way towards the Congress building, leading to violent confrontations with the police.

This pattern of repetitive street protests is very similar to that which characterised the Great French Revolution of 1789-1794, with its *journées*—days when the population of the poorer parts of Paris would swarm from the streets towards symbols of power in the city centre. A 21st century uprising was taking the form of the archetypical 18th century revolution!

After the first successful spontaneous uprising people began to see the need to organise themselves. Sections of the media were attempting to give the impression everything was over, claiming everyone had gone to the beaches (it was, being in the southern hemisphere, high summer). Others painted a picture of the middle classes living in terror of mobs of poor people invading their homes and stealing their belongings (reminiscent of 'the great fear' of the French Revolution). And some of the most powerful trade union leaders had thrown their weight behind the government and were trying to isolate the protests. Meanwhile, there were real problems with relying simply on spontaneous action. There were cases of the unemployed and the hungry poor attacking not only the large supermarkets and agribusinesses, but also small shopkeepers and street traders nearly as poor as themselves, which risked driving them into the arms of the government. The young people who bore the brunt of the fighting with the police could easily end up isolated from the mass of demonstrators, making it easier for the secret services to engage in provocations designed to justify repressive measures. Finally, there was also a need to prevent Peronist leaders in the government resorting to an old trick of mobilising 'lumpenproletarian' mobs to attack protesters for 30 to 50 pesos a day.

People began to get together in 'popular assemblies', as a Buenos Aires newspaper from one of the poorer parts of the city reported:

> *They are residents of* ***San Cristóbal****. 'In the last weeks we've been between euphoria and fear', they say. 'We have done things which we never even thought of and we still don't know what else we'll have to do.' They met up on the corner of* ***La Rioja*** *and* ***San Juan*** *for the protests against de la Rua and marched to the Congress, and they got together the next day to denounce the repression. They made another* ***cacerolazo*** *when the Legislative Assembly appointed Duhalde. On the Sunday 150 people responded to a call to meet in the* ***Plaza Martin Ferro*** *and organised an impromptu assembly. Now they have decided on a more stable form of organisation 'apart from the parties'.*
>
> *Among them were 'a priest, various housewives, two members of the Communist Party, a member of the Workers Party, a bar owner, half a dozen unemployed people…the local leaders of the Peronist party, various social psychologists, university students and a group of workers from the nearby hospital'. 'We are drawing up a list of all the unemployed in the neighour-hood,' said one. Others tell, 'We are taking care of security, because there were unknown people on the last* ***cacerolazo****,' and, 'We are calling a new* ***cacerolazo*** *against the rising prices'.*[46]

Soon assemblies like this were blossoming right across greater Buenos Aires and in dozens of provincial centres. A description by a journalist for the French paper *Libération* has provided a sense of the atmosphere at them, in a well-to-do neighbourhood:

> *It's 11pm at the crossroads of the avenues* ***Cabildo*** *and* ***Congreso****. With a mega-phone in his hand a man of about 30 tries to get some order. 'We are going to proceed to a vote on the ideas formulated this evening'—non-payment of the foreign debt and an inquiry into its legitimacy, nationalisation of the banks, revisions of the contracts with the foreign enterprises running the public ser-vices, whose abusive behaviour has exasperated everyone. This Monday they had been meeting for three hours. Twenty people have spoken. A chair has tried to restrict them to two minutes, but most have exceeded that. They are not activists of any party. They have come with a single banner which has stopped*

*the traffic: 'The Popular Assembly of* ***Belgrano*** *district'.*

*For a month this scene has been repeated every evening, from Monday to Saturday in one or other district of the city. And on Sunday, there are around 5,000 people in the* ***Centenario*** *park for the mother of all assemblies, which brings together people from the whole city. From these popular assemblies was born the first* ***cacerolazo*** *on a national scale which brought tens of thousands of people onto the roads of all the big cities.*[47]

A journalist for the Mexican left wing daily *La Jornada* paints a similar picture:

*Dozens of district assemblies are functioning, a genuine product of the popular organisation that grew out of the rebellion of the* ***cacerolas****. They are demanding the truth about the situation and punishment for those responsible as the anger grows against the foreign banks and privatisation. In these assemblies they are talking today of the '10 billion that the electricity companies Edenor and Edesur have taken, of $800 to $1,000 million dollars of profits made each year by the telephone companies'.*[48]

A participant at one of the city-wide assemblies in the *Centenario* park reports:

*There were about 6,000 people there, from more or less 80 neighbourhood committees from the city and the suburbs and including the* ***piqueteros****. The slogans reflected the maturity of the demands of the different assemblies and the necessity of constructing bigger channels of popular feeling, independent of the political apparatuses.*[49]

The demands included non-payment of the foreign debt, nationalisation of privatised enterprises under the control of workers and the neighbourhood committees, punishment of those responsible for repression on 19-20 December and 25 January, establishment of security committees at both the district and the city level to deal with police attempts at provocation in assemblies and demonstrations, support for the unemployed *piqueteros*, the calling of a national congress of *piquetero* organisations and popular assemblies, support for the struggles of railway, telecommunications and textile workers, and criticism of the behaviour of the union leaders in not backing these.

Similar gatherings were taking place in numerous provincial towns, big and small—in Córdoba, in Neuquén, in the small Tucumán towns, in Mercedes, in La Plata, in Olavarria, to name just a few.[50] And in each case, they were not mere talking shops. Their discussions were about local activities—demanding medicines for the local pharmacies, supporting workers fighting to keep their plants open, going to supermarkets to demand food, going to the banks to insist on payment for public sector employees, protesting against repressive measures, as well as raising again and again the demands for renationalisation of the privatised concerns, action against the banks, and opposition to the *corralito*.

The neighbourhood committees and popular assemblies express the need of those who have overthrown presidents to organise themselves. They are the form taken by the mass, popular repudiation of the old order. In this respect they have certain similarities with the characteristic forms of mass self organisation that arose in the great working class struggles of the 20th century—the workers' councils or soviets. But they also have very important differences from these.

First, the popular assemblies are not yet bodies of delegates. The people at them represent themselves, but do not have an organic connection with some group of people who they represent—and who can recall them if they do not carry out their will. Second, they draw together people from very different class backgrounds, as is shown by the fact that there are neighbourhood committees in the prosperous parts of Buenos Aires like *Belgrano* and *Libertador* as well as in working and lower middle class areas.

Finally, the popular assemblies are not anchored in the workplaces where millions of Argentinians are still drawn together on a daily basis to toil. They are mainly collections of individuals from the localities and the various *piqueteros* organisations of unemployed workers. Reports tell that in some of the assemblies an important leading role is played by unemployed activists shaped by their role in past industrial struggles—the CCC banner of the *Corriente Clasista y Combativa* (Combative Class Current) features in many of the protests. But this does not make them into an organic expression of Argentinia's working class with its long and militant history. They are, in fact, closer to the *sections*—the nightly district mass meetings—of the French Revolution than to the workers' councils of 1905 and 1917 in Russia, November 1918 in Germany, or October and November 1956 in Hungary.

There is another, linked feature of the popular assemblies and the *cacerolazos*. Although the demands they raise challenge the whole structures of Argentinian capitalism, much of their language is not anti-capitalist, still less socialist. Instead, it focuses on the one hand on the corruption of the political elite—those leading the two mainstream political parties, the supreme court, the generals—and on the other on the pernicious role of foreign capital in privatisation. The language is nationalist, the most frequent banner the national flag, the most popular chorus that of the national anthem.

To understand these features, it is necessary to look at the historical development of the Argentinian working class movement.

## Peronism and the unions

Peronism dominated the Argentinian working class movement for more than half a century after 1945 much as Labourism dominated the British working class movement. It had not always been so. At the time of the *Semana Trágica* in 1919 there were very powerful anarchist, syndicalist and reformist socialist currents, and from the early 1920s to the early 1940s Communism was a significant force. But from then on Peronism was dominant.

Juan Peron himself was influenced by the 'corporatist' notions of Italian fascism (he spent two years in Mussolini's Italy and was in exile in Franco's Spain in the 1960s). But the movement he built was certainly not fascist. In the years 1943-1945 he managed to put together a formula which appealed to sections of workers, sections of the bourgeoisie and parts of the state machine alike. It shifted resources from the agrarian sector into the building of industrial firms catering for a protected domestic market while conceding to many of the demands of an already militant working class. And it was able to portray this as a struggle of the whole Argentinian 'nation' against a parasitic 'oligarchy' tied to 'imperialism'. This enabled him to take over the trade union bureaucracy from its old Communist or Socialist leaders, either buying them off or imposing his own people in their place, with the acquiescence of the workers.

The formula was wearing a little thin by the time the military ousted Peron in 1955 against a background of falling working class living standards. But the attacks on workers' organisation under the succession of non-Peronist governments over the next 17 years reinforced its hold. The Peron period seemed like a golden age compared with what followed. And the image of Peronism as a working class political force was strengthened by the fact that the trade union bureaucracy was the centre of organised Peronism for the 17 years during which the Peronist party was banned. For the great majority of Argentinian workers, Peronism was the working class movement in those years. The majority of the battles they waged against a succession of military and civil governments were battles waged under its banner.

Yet it remained a cross-class alliance dominated by the requirements of a section of Argentinian capitalism. Politically it represented a middle bourgeoisie, which benefited from a protected market, and the bureaucrats running the big new state industries and banks, as well as the union bureaucracy. The union bureaucracy itself was from the beginning corrupt, its individual members often enjoying lucrative connections with the other elements within Peronism. But it still had to fight for its position. So its behaviour was not just bureaucratic. It could see the need on occasions to use carefully controlled but very militant—and sometimes very violent—actions so as to assert its own interests and make sure it kept workers' allegiance. It was, in some respects, more like a corrupt US union like the Teamsters during the reign of Jimmy Hoffa than the British TUC, except it played a much more central role in mainstream bourgeois politics.

The second period of Peronist rule, from 1973, came close to tearing the political movement apart. A new generation of students and young workers had given their own revolutionary interpretation to Peronism during the bitter repression of the Onganía dictatorship of the late 1960s. They saw Peron's nationalism as one of a kind with that of the Cuban revolution, Che Guevara and the Vietnamese liberation struggle, and interpreted the struggle of workers in Argentina as part of a national struggle against imperialism (even though the Argentinian bourgeoisie had long enjoyed national independence, there were no foreign bases and little foreign capital). This led the armed left wing Peronist youth, the Monteneros, to throw their weight behind strikes, occupations and clashes with the forces of the state. But once Peronism was back in power, the bourgeois forces within it and the political bosses linked to them increasingly looked to repress the workers' movement and the left. By 1974-1975 Lopez Vega, the key minister in Isabel Peron's government, was organising armed bands (the AAA Anti-Communist Alliance) to murder trade union militants and leftists, including those still formally within the ranks of Peronism. The trade union bureaucracy was caught between welcoming the attacks on the left and needing to maintain its hold over the working class—and its own standing in relation to the ruling class—by making certain militant gestures (like calling the first ever general strike against a Peronist government in 1975).

The crisis within Peronism allowed other political forces to begin to have an impact. 'Classist' currents, which looked to the working class, not an alliance with 'patriotic employers', were important in 'new' industries like those in Córdoba. Maoists developed influence in a few local unions. A Trotskyist organisation which had entered Peronism broke away with several thousand members, before itself splitting between a Guevarist wing, the PRT/ERP, centred around guerrilla warfare and with considerable influence in places like Córdoba, and a rival party, the PST, oriented to work within the unions.[51]

Yet the influence of Peronism persisted. It did so because Peronism was the main Argentinian form of reformism, even if it was a reformism rather different to European social democracy. Workers without the confidence to take on and defeat capitalism through their own efforts looked to the Peronists to do limited things for them within the existing system. They would not shift their allegiance entirely until they found a revolutionary political force that could lead them to at least limited victories. Hence the paradoxical reality that the very defeats brought about by Peronist leadership could lead workers to lose confidence and so continue to rely on such leadership.

The onslaught on the left helped the Peronist bureaucracy after the coup of 1976. Rank and file militancy was literally decimated—estimates suggest that 10,000 out of 100,000 shop stewards were murdered during the military dictatorship. The bureaucracy remained more or less intact, maintaining contacts with the leading generals, and was able to re-establish an open national presence and then to make a gesture to the economic bitterness of ordinary trade unionists by calling one-day general strikes.

After the fall of the junta, opposition lists won elections in certain unions, but the influence of Peronist ideas on the working class as a whole was strong enough at the end of the 1980s for people to see the election of Menem in 1989 as a great victory. As a study of workers' struggle in the Buenos Aires shipyards reports:

> *In this moment, the great majority of workers believed that Peronism in power would mean a return to the epoch when the workers received 47 percent of the national income and could have a job and wage that allowed them to survive... In the shipyards, even the most militant sectors did not lose all their illusions in the bourgeois parties, the trade union hierarchy, and the laws and the justice of the employers.*[52]

These illusions allowed Menem and Cavallo to push through privatisation and restructuring without facing co-ordinated resistance. There were explosions of bitterness, with strikes and occupations over factory closures and redundancies. But these were usually isolated explosions, followed by defeat and demoralisation. All the time there was pressure on workers to work harder, with the management openly threatening to close plants if they did not. In these circumstances the carrot of redundancy payments had a similar effect to, say, that in Britain in the 1980s. Many workers who saw little hope of saving everyone's job through collective resistance opted to take the bribe.

So in the militant shipyard of *Astilleros de Rio Santiago* thousands of workers ended up accepting voluntary redundancy in the year 1981. One of the activists admits, 'The voluntary redundancy was a temptation for everyone, including me'.[53] The Marxist historian of the Argentinian labour movement Pablo Pozzi writes, 'Unable to find other employment, laid off workers set up small businesses, such as newspaper stands, vegetable and grocery stores. For instance, between the years 1988 and 1994, the number of taxi cabs in Buenos Aires increased from 36,000 to 55,000'.[54]

Those workers who kept their jobs became more dependent than before on the meagre protection provided them by their union membership. But lacking the confidence to take struggles into their own hands, this meant dependencc on the union bureaucracies. Even when it came to redundancy, it was better to have bad redundancy terms negotiated by the union bureaucrats than deplorable ones imposed by the employer without any negotiation. Sections of the union bureaucracy did feel compelled to distance themselves from the government and split from the main CGT. But this was not the same as giving a lead to mass struggle.

Even when workers finally lost faith in Menem in the mid-1990s, many retained illusions in his former vice-president, Duhalde, now governor of Buenos Aires. He used his position to try to distance himself from the central government and so, for instance, 'created illusions in the immense majority of the shipyard workers'.[55]

At this time Duhalde was also trying to create his own Peronist political apparatus apart from the unions through 'a neighbourhood provincial network structured around the *manzaneras* (women block leaders). These women served as a conduit for government aid and as a connection for political favours... They served as an element of neighbourhood control and political mobilisation'.[56] Even in recent weeks, reports suggest Duhalde had enough influence in some of the poorer parts of the city to pay 'lumpenproletarian' groups to mobilise on his behalf, initially against the de la Rua government and then against the left.

The bitter experience of the 1990s did shake the hold of Peronism over organised workers. By the end of the decade there were three rival trade union federations—the official CGT, firmly in the hands of old-style bureaucrats, a rival dissident CGT-*combatiente*, standing a little apart from official Peronism, and the CTA, verbally inclined towards the left. But the methods of these rival federations were not fundamentally different to that of the 'official' CGT. They called occasional strikes to put pressure on the employers and the government, but they did not attempt to maintain sustained struggles in defence of their members. In 1997 the CTA was able to involve about 40 percent of the country's workers in a general strike, creating an atmosphere in which it was not long before the CGT had to call for such action against the Menem government. But its leaders still saw their main function as to exert pressure on those in power and campaigned electorally for the bourgeois Radical-*Frepaso* coalition.[57]

The limitations of all the union federations were shown in last December's events. There was a general strike on 13 December. But the unions took no action in the crucial days after that, so that as an organised force workers simply were not present on 19-20 December. Only when the government was already on its last legs on 20 December did the CTA announce a general strike for the next day—a strike which was called off after the government fell. And in the days that followed, instead of taking the head of the anti-government feeling among the vast mass of the population, the CGT leaders met with Rodriguez Saá and proclaimed him as one of them, a 'Peronist of the old sort'.

Since then the CTA federation has given support to some protests, and so have some local union bodies. But the two main federations have continued to stand apart from the protests, attempting to isolate the millions of workers who still hold jobs, however precariously, from the movement that has been sweeping the streets and the neighbourhoods.

## The bitter decade

The rising was spontaneous. It would be absurd to claim otherwise.[58] But that does not mean that there were no currents of opposition that prepared the ground for it. The bitter attempts by workers to stop closures and impose redundancies through the 1990s may have been defeated, but they kept alive a spirit of resistance, in the face of which even the hard-nosed neo-liberals in the Menem government had to make occasional concessions. The one-day general strikes called by the union bureaucracy may have usually had an almost ritualistic character, without pickets or demonstrations. But they did bring large swathes of industry and transport to a standstill, showing that there was a power that could paralyse the country. They also forced the neo-liberals to back off from certain of their demands (as when Cavallo resigned in 1996 when he wanted to cut family allowances and salaries).[59] Those who dismiss these strikes out of hand fail to grasp the simple fact that they showed the potential power of the workers, despite their passivity.[60]

Along with these 'old' forms of struggle, new ones began to arise. Already, the economic crisis of 1989 saw the first spontaneous riots:

> *In 1989 the people in the Patagonian province of Chubut mobilised for a week to get rid of a governor. Later, in June of that year, thousands of people in Buenos Aires and Rosario rioted, sacking supermarkets and grocery stores. Over the next two years neighbours in different cities and towns took to the streets several times... By 1993 the riots had turned more violent, with people attacking (and burning down) the government house in north western Santiago del Estero province, as well as in Jujuy,* ***La Rioja****, Chaco, Tucumán, and Corrientes. The main characteristic of these riots was the unexpectedness, the fact that they happened quickly, lasting rarely more than a day, and left no visible forms of organisation. In a sense, they were more a catharsis for accumulated anger and frustration than a new form of struggle. Though violent and pervasive, they were relatively easy to control. In all cases the government attempted to ignore the upheaval, hoping it would die down, and when it didn't its response included repression by security forces.*[61]

In the first part of the 1990s these local near-uprisings were short lived and isolated from each other. They also did not lead to any permanent organisation. This began to change by 1996. A series of struggles in Neuquén province, in Patagonia, were symptomatic of the new trend:

> ***Cutral Có** and **Plaza Huincul** are two townships in the upper Patagonian Neuquén province, with some 55,000 inhabitants...built and developed around the petroleum industry... YPF (the state oil firm) was privatised between 1994 and 1995, with over 80 percent of its employees being laid off as a result. By 1996 the townships had a 35.7 percent unemployment rate, and 23,500 persons were below the poverty line. By June 1996, the local governor had failed to sign an agreement with a Canadian corporation to establish a fertiliser plant in the area, and the local population took to the streets. Local shopkeepers closed their doors, and all over the two towns barricades were set up manned by some 5,000 residents. Those people manning the barricades became known as the **piqueteros** (pickets). Security forces besieged the entrenched townspeople.*[62]

The governor of the province managed to end the unrest after a week by promising negotiations with a committee of townspeople and subsidies for the poorest families. But struggle erupted again nine months later during a teachers' strike against redundancies and salary cuts. The nearby highways were blocked, leading to clashes between the police and youths armed with sticks and slings, with the police killing one woman.

In this period there were similar such protests and clashes in Tartagal and Jujuy in the north west, and La Plata and Buenos Aires on the coast: 'National highways were blockaded by pickets, students demonstrated and confronted the police, workers and farmers went on strike... The uprisings had an effect on the popular imagination... Each new conflict helped set off others. Innovations in modes of struggle spread from one to the other'.[63] What is more, new ways of organising the struggle were also emerging. Typically they were run by popular assemblies, mass meetings at which all those involved in the action could take part. This was very different from the bureaucratic chains of command which characterised the unions in all three union federations.

There was a brief lull in the spread of such struggles in 1997-1998, as people expected some improvement in their situation from elections. But disappointment soon led to them arising on an even bigger scale. There were major movements in the city of Nequén, General Mosconi, La Esperanza, Jujuy, Cipolletti, Oran, Bahia Blanca, Comodoro Rivadavia. In Tartagal, near Salta, in the far north west, people attacked the police station.[64] In the second half of 2000 the movement of the unemployed intersected for the first time with a mass mobilisation of employed workers. In the Buenos Aires suburb of *Matanza*, with its 2 million population and the country's biggest concentration of industry in the 1970s, 1,000 unemployed *piqueteros* blocked a major highway for a week. A second wave of struggle in Tartagal brought together the unemployed and transport workers who blocked the roads. When the police shot a demonstrator dead, people occupied a police station, took the police officers hostage and seized their arms.[65]

The different movements came together again, on an even bigger scale, the following March (2001) in the popular upsurge that led to the resignation of Lopéz Murphy from the government and his replacement by Cavallo. The announcement of massive cuts in the education budget led to a wave of struggle among students (although still led by the youth branch of the governmental Radical Party), a 48-hour strike by teachers, a march by the unemployed organisations on Buenos Aires and then a 24-hour general strike by all three union federations. 'The strikes, the occupations of universities, the general discontent created a very difficult situation for the government', wrote the commentator Pasquini Duran in the daily *Página 12*, 'The economic options available had to take into account an essential fact—society had said "Enough!"... For the first time for a long time, the politicos feared civil disobedience more than the markets'.[66]

The unemployed movement continued to grow from May to August 2001, with two national conferences of the *piquetero* organisations and the shutting down of 300 major highways by tens of thousands of pickets. Clashes with the police killed five pickets.[67] Analysing the March crisis, the Argentinian Marxist Roberto Saenz quite rightly noted:

> *We can say that a new cycle of struggles has started which has features very distinct from these prevailing in the struggles of the past decade. Everything is being questioned. In the population there is a state of permanent debate... There is a new vanguard developing within the popular layers, which is beginning to acquire certain features, above all within the unemployed movements, but also among sections of the employed... The new movements arise in general outside the old traditional trade union organisations, with direct democracy from below and new leaders.*[68]

The new forces and the new forms of struggle, then, were already showing in March last year that they could shake society to its roots—and this at a time when the ruling class was increasingly split over what to do about the acute financial crisis of both Argentinian industry and the state. That is why those on the Marxist left who spoke then about the development of a potentially revolutionary (or 'pre-revolutionary') situation were correct.

This did not mean, however, that the consciousness of those leading the new movements was itself automatically, or even generally, revolutionary. Different people who got involved brought with them different conceptions of how to fight, and also different expectations of what could be achieved. This was shown by the early struggle in Neuquén province. The militant youths who fought physically against the police were bitterly angry when the main local leaders agreed to a compromise with the governor that provided a few jobs and a few subsidies for the very hard up. The same sorts of divisions expressed themselves in the major movement in *Matanza*. Its leaders agreed after a week of blocking the road to call it off in return for 'job plans' doing public works for 7,500 out of the hundreds of thousands unemployed in the district. A minority of protesters were not happy with this, but did not have the confidence to challenge the existing leaders.[69]

The fact that people are unemployed does not automatically stop them attempting to find remedies within the existing system. What motivated most people to join the protests was the desire to deal with the immediate, desperate situation. So it was that major tendencies with the *piqueteros* movement looked to pressurising the government for small improvement, like 'job plans', rather than to an apparently distant chance of social revolution. This was true of the major forces involved in the *Matanza* struggle—the MTA union and the *Corriente Clasista y Combativa*. It was also true of those who dominated the national meetings of the *piqueteros* in the summer of 2001. But simply demanding 'job plans' could play into the government's hands. It could promise such things and then hope to go back on its promises once the immediate protests were over. And it could also expect the implementation of such schemes to draw some of the unemployed activists into its own patronage networks. One critic pointed out, 'The political clientism created around the miserable pay that is to be got for cutting weeds or painting kerbs benefits most the bosses of the various political parties who negotiate with the hunger and poverty of the unemployed'.[70] Such tendencies mean that it is quite wrong to romanticise the unemployed movements and contrast them as 'genuinely revolutionary' in contraposition to the employed workers in the workplaces.

The media and the mainstream parties may have created prejudices against the unemployed among those with jobs, claiming them to be lazy and not interested in work. But the movements of 2000-2001 showed the possibilities of linking the unemployed movements and the most militant sections of employed workers. For instance, an important part was played in the organisation of the *Matanza* protest by workers sacked from a refrigeration plant and former trade union militants. And workers from important workplaces sent delegations to provide material help to the blockaders.[71]

Despite the scale of the struggles last year, neither the employed nor the unemployed sections of the working class had broken with the idea that their demands could somehow be fulfilled within the present system. Brought up within the present system and knowing no other, they tended to continue to take it for granted, at the same time as their own struggles were running directly counter to its requirements. Or to put it another way, they wanted one thing in practice, another in terms of the old ideas that still existed in their heads. This 'contradictory consciousness' (to use Gramsci's term) encouraged a continued tendency towards reformism. Not surprisingly, there seems to have been a certain rise of new versions of left reformism just as the struggles were piling one on top of the other. So opinion polls showed one of the most popular politicians at the time to be Elisa Carrió, a former Radical Party MP who had switched to opposition to the de la Rua government. And even some of the militant organisations involved in organising the *piqueteros* still seem to look to an alliance with supposedly anti neo-liberal sections of 'national', 'productive' capital.

The tendency of people to look for reformist options will not have disappeared, despite the successes of the popular movement on the streets. In every great revolutionary upheaval there is a double trend. Those who have been militant in the past tend to move further to the left until they begin to break with old reformist nostrums. But millions of new people move into action for the first time, and they tend initially to identify with prominent political figures who seem radical but not 'unrealistically' revolutionary. In the Russian Revolution of 1917, the overwhelming majority in the soviets immediately after the February revolution backed the Provisional Government. In the German Revolution of 1918-1919, the mass of workers and soldiers initially put their faith in the social democrats, not the *Spartakusbund* of Rosa Luxemburg and Karl Liebknecht. In the Portuguese Revolution of 1974-1975, the mass of workers looked either to the reformist Communist Party or to the even more reformist Socialist Party, and only a small minority to the revolutionary left.

## The revolutionary left

James Petras has claimed in a widely circulated article that the revolutionary left was nowhere to be seen in the events of 19-20 December.[72] Fortunately, the claim is by no means wholly true. Some sections of the revolutionary left were present on the day[73] and have thrown themselves into attempting to build and influence the popular committees since.[74] What is true, however, is that the Argentinian far left is small in size, split into several different groups, and possesses nothing like the standing to influence a mass spontaneous uprising.

The left was not always so weak. Although the repression of the junta was disproportionately directed against the far left, killing a large number of its activists and forcing many more into exile, it was still a substantial force in the late 1980s. The Trotskyist organisation the MAS (formed in 1983 by a merger of the old PST with various other socialist groups) then had several thousand members, and another group, the *Partido Obrero*, seems to have been quite sizeable. But the years of defeat for the workers' movement began to exact a toll by the end of the decade. The overall trajectory was not that different to that of much of the European left. Pablo Pozzi tells:

> *Though* [thc organised left] *grew significantly between 1983 and 1986, it was hurt by the 1976-1983 repression, the collapse of the Soviet Union and the overall international situation. The disappearance without a whimper of the USSR demoralised many activists, including those who had traditionally criticised Stalinism... In addition, to many people it implied that socialism was no longer on the agenda, if it had ever been. This opened up a lot of possibilist notions, including several social democratic variants. The road to socialism suddenly became not revolution but rather an evolution of ever-increasing democratic spaces to be acquired through electoral participation...*
>
> *After 1983 most leftist organisations launched themselves into the electoral struggle hoping to elect a few legislators. Many leftist groups spent their scarce resources and their activists in elections, pulling them away from mass work. A lot of energy was spent in forming electoral alliances and efforts were made to become acceptable to the press and the mainstream voter... MAS succeeded in electing a national Congressman, a local councillor and a provincial deputy, but the cost was high... The notion emerged within the party that participation in mass struggles imperilled further electoral advances, for it alienated the middle classes.*[75]

MAS eventually split into several fragments, with the group that kept the name turning back towards a revolutionary perspective which talks of 'socialism or barbarism' and 'socialism from below'. Alongside it are the *Partido Obrero* (Workers Party)—also quite large in the late 1980s. There also exists another fragment of the old MAS, the Movement for Socialism (MST), the smaller and more recently formed *Partido do los Trabajadores por el Socialismo* (Party of Workers for Socialism), and the supposedly Maoist *Partido Comunista Revolucionario* (influential in the *Corriente Clasista y Combativa*). These all retain some worker militants from the 1970s and 1980s, but between them they have nothing like the impact of the far left of a dozen years ago.

The Communist Party likewise suffered both a loss of influence and internal fragmentation. In 1989 it had formed an electoral alliance with MAS. In 1993, however, it looked to Peronist politicians who had been cast aside by Menem's government. But the key figure in this alliance then drove it out and became part of the *Frepaso* coalition, joining the de la Rua government that was swept away on 19-20 December.[76]

Finally, the atmosphere of those years encouraged attempts to find some sort of reformist alternative to the crisis. The notion that neo-liberalism was simply a crazy policy imposed on 'the whole country' by foreign capital and its local stooge Cavallo, rather than reflecting the needs of Argentinian capital to climb onto the world stage, led the CTA, for instance, to hunt for a section of local capitalism which would join it in a programme of national expansion based upon boosting workers' incomes and the market for consumer goods.[77]

The early and mid-1990s was a very difficult period for those sections of the left that survived, just as the years in Britain after the defeat of the miners' strike (1984-1985) and the print workers' fight (1986-1987) were extremely difficult. And they inevitably created two apparently contradictory but in reality complementary tendencies on the left.

The first tendency was to accommodation, if not with neo-liberalism (which did occur in some cases), at least with various reformist schemes—encouraged in Argentina by the old left habit of seeing the main enemy as being foreign capital, against which it was necessary to ally with sections of local capital. For activists who managed to maintain their jobs in organised workplaces, there was the parallel pressure to accommodate to the methods of the union bureaucracy, substituting verbal opposition to its politics for the very difficult task of mobilising struggle in face of resistance from it.

The second tendency was sectarianism. Rarely able to move real forces in opposition to the attacks of the system, it was very tempting for left groups try to substitute programmatic formulas for this—and then to argue vehemently with each other about the details of the formulas. Demands like that for a 'constituent assembly' were endowed with magical qualities they have never possessed (even in those historic situations when they were appropriate). Along with this often went a tendency to use verbal abuse against reformist currents and the trade union bureaucracy rather than methods of argument that could win over those workers who still looked to them. This must be an impediment to providing the sort of practical leadership that the movement needs today.

Yet the left should have the possibility of having an impact on events. Provincial elections took place in October 2001. Their most notable feature was the disaffection with the mainstream political parties shown by the huge level of abstention and spoiled votes—nearly 10 million—in a country where voting is supposedly compulsory. But some of the disaffected showed a willingness to look to left wing alternatives. The combined national vote of the various left parties and groups was over 1 million—of which 500,000 went to the joint Communist Party/Socialist Workers

Movement (MST) list, 250,000 to the joint Workers Party (PO)/Movement Towards Socialism (MAS) list, and 100,000 to the Party of Workers for Socialism (PTS). In Buenos Aires city the left got a hefty 27 percent of the vote, and it also did well in cities like Córdoba and Salta.

The vote for the left seems mainly to have been a protest vote, rather than a sign of deep agreement with its positions. It showed there is potential for the left to be an influence, that there are people prepared to look to socialist politics as an alternative to those of the rival bourgeois parties, but no more than that. The question since 19-20 December is whether the revolutionary left can build on that potential.

## The crisis for the ruling class

In a famous passage Lenin argued that for a revolutionary situation to exist it is not good enough for the exploited class to find conditions insufferable. The ruling class also has to reach the conclusion that things cannot continue in the old way. This creates deep, paralysing splits within it, throwing the whole of society into turmoil, and spurring the exploited classes to express their own anger.

This was already clear in the crisis of March last year, which saw the ousting of Lopéz Murphy and his replacement by Cavallo. When Lopéz Murphy announced his plan for savage cuts in the education system he was cheered to the rafters by a gathering of 300 top business people. But at the same time the UIA (roughly equivalent to the Institute of Directors in Britain) criticised the scheme. The return of Cavallo to the economics ministry briefly quelled such disagreements, but they had returned in a stronger form by the summer. The issue in dispute within the capitalist class was whether the way out of the crisis lay in devaluing the peso (so, hopefully cutting imports and raising exports) or replacing it once and for all by the US dollar (so making foreign investors more 'confident' that they could safely lend to Argentina).

Behind this argument over monetary policy lay a clash of real material interests. Dollarisation represented a way of protecting wealth from the Argentinian crisis for those financial sectors that had reaped hard cash out of the previous ten years, and for the very rich. It translated it into a form that could be moved anywhere in the world in search of more profits. By contrast, those who owned productive industries—including even foreign firms that had bought up those industries with privatisation—wanted to escape from being tied to the dollar. Neo-liberalism had suited them in the early 1990s when it led to smaller firms being driven out of business and a concentration of assets in their own hands. The destruction of certain 'uncompetitive' industries was, for them, a price worth paying for creating a lean Argentinian capitalism with much reduced labour costs. But the ability of the remaining industries to sell their goods in the face of foreign competition was undermined by the high value of the peso so long as it was linked one for one to the dollar. Devaluation, they believed, would reduce the prices for which they could sell goods abroad, while staunching the flow of imports and raising the prices they could charge at home. So manufacturing firms and the big agribusinesses opposed dollarisation and pressed for devaluation.

The crisis of ruling class politics became acute when the IMF refused to release more funds in December and the banking system threatened to grind to a halt. The two mainstream political parties, the Radicals and the Peronists, were increasingly fragmented internally, with the various local Peronist political bosses intent on pursuing measures to bolster their individual positions with little concern for the interests of the ruling class as a whole. No political figure was powerful enough to impose either dollarisation or devaluation. There was drift without any policy except more budget cuts until the shortage of dollars compelled the government to freeze bank accounts with the *corralito*—and seal its own fate.

The eruption of the masses onto the political scene increased the level of fragmentation. Rival politicians had to respond not just to the prompting of the warring sections of the ruling class, but also to the pressure from below. They knew that saying the wrong thing and upsetting the crowds could ruin political reputations—a popular gesture, on the other hand, might set them off on amazing careers. In this way the tumult in the streets also became tumult in the Congress and the presidential *Casa Rosada* ('Pink House'). Rodriguez Saá was appointed president by the political establishment, only to be overthrown just over a week later after further mass insurgency on the streets and political plotting by his rivals among the Peronist bosses. Duhalde, one of the chief plotters, took his place, but seemed unable to produce a coherent programme. He announced the devaluation of the currency and a moratorium (temporary halt) to payments on the foreign debt, but wasted a month elaborating what this meant for the billions of pesos deposited in and owed to the banks. Meanwhile the *corralito* remained in effect, and with it the bitterness of the middle classes. The government denounced 'the monstrous evasion of the tax system, characterised by the punishment of consumers and the lowest level of taxation on profits in the world' and sent the police in to inspect the books of banks suspected of moving funds abroad.[78] But it also hastened to assure the foreign owners of privatised concerns that it was not going to damage their interests and initiated discussions with the IMF on debt payments.

*Financial Times* columnist Martin Wolf summed up the dismay among many capitalist interests at the disarray within the government. 'Argentina's president' had 'turned calamity into something worse' by his efforts at a 'populist' policy aimed at pleasing everyone.[79] Wolf did not say what else Duhalde could do if he was to save his political head.

A week later the previously warring sections of big Argentinian capitalism came together to put pressure on Duhalde to drop the 'populism'. A headline in *Página 12* read 'The Holy Alliance Of The 90s Is Reborn'. The story underneath told of a coming together of 'the association of Argentinian banks and the most powerful business interests' now that the issue of devaluation had been settled: 'Since devaluation, the banks and the great national economic groups like Pérez Companc, Techint, Macri, Fortabat and Bulgheroni have identified common interests and rearmed the society formed in the 1990s. The fight of the Union Industrial and the men of construction and the agrarian interests against the profiteers of the last decade has come to its end'.[80]

Even this did not spell the end of political infighting among those who had presided over neo-liberalisation. The very day this report appeared, the Supreme Court intervened to declare the *corralito* illegal. The court is dominated by people handpicked by Menem during his presidency, and is widely seen as linked, via him, to powerful and dubious business interests. The move was clearly a manoeuvre aimed at destabilising the Duhalde government. As huge crowds once again swarmed through the centre of Buenos Aires, Duhalde announced a new scheme for slowly unfreezing bank accounts and parliamentarians talked of impeaching the Supreme Court. The *Financial Times* correspondent believed this could 'set the stage for the most serious constitutional crisis since the country returned to democracy in 1983'.[81] In the days that followed 'rumours about a military or civil-military coup began to circulate, so weakening the government even further'.[82]

The government's measures for dealing with the banking crisis were exacerbating social tensions. It tried to give the measures a populist appeal by saying they would centre around unfreezing bank accounts sufficiently for people to withdraw amounts each month equal to their wages or pensions. But it rapidly became clear more was involved.

At a time when the dollar was worth about 1.8 pesos on the exchanges, the government had agreed to restrict the amount that needed to be paid back to the banks by large debtors (those with more than $100,000 dollars of debt) to one peso for each dollar of debt, and to compensate the banks for the difference. In effect, it was 'statifying' the debt of the giant financial and industrial concerns.[83] At the same time, those with savings in the banks were only to get 1.4 pesos for each dollar saved. In practice, small savers were going to join with the state in subsidising large debtors. This would, for instance, halve the real level of the $350 million debt of the firm Pérez Companc, and at the same time increase the indebtedness of the state by an estimated $7 billion.[84]

The deal was much more favourable to big capital than that originally envisaged by Duhalde's economy minister Remes Lenicov. But the 'Economic and Bank groups' with the 'indirect help of the Supreme Court, which brought the Duhalde government to the verge of collapse', persuaded the government to introduce the measures in their final form.[85] It was not only small savers who were hit. In fact in the next few days prices began to rise right across the board, with medicines (both home produced and imported) shooting up by 35 percent overnight.

Finally, the government was also seeking further agreement with the International Monetary Fund, and promising further cuts in public spending to achieve it. This can only push the economy further into recession at a time of rising prices.

Not surprisingly, the days after the announcement of these measures have seen no decrease in social tensions. Employees who still have jobs will be forced to struggle to maintain the real value of their earnings in the face of rapid inflation and to defend their jobs as the recession gets deeper. The pressures driving the unemployed into abject poverty will get greater. And there will be great resentment among small savers at having to subsidise the big capitalists. A report from Buenos Aires tells:

> *Each day the movement of the popular assemblies is gaining more force. The open meetings, the neighbourhood assemblies and the multi-sector gatherings have spread to almost all the provincial capitals and are beginning to take in, through the actions of the* ***piqueteros****, wide zones of the Buenos Aires conurbation (above all in the areas adjoining the capital, like* ***Matanza****,* ***Valentin Alsina*** *and* ***Tres de Febrero****, which have been bastions of the Duhaldist apparatus), which, as you can imagine, is worrying the Justicialist Party machine in Buenos Aires. On the last demonstration you could see the tendency for the popular assemblies to converge with the movement of the* ***piqueteros****, chanting the same slogans ('****Piquete y cacerola!*** *The struggle is the same!' 'Work for everyone', 'Get rid of them all, don't let a single one remain') and marching together to the* ***Plaza de Mayo****.*

## Where is Argentina going?

The economic and political instability of Argentina make it impossible to predict what will happen next. The government desperately wants to deflate the *cacerolazo* protests, by detaching sections of the middle class from the movements of the poor and the unemployed. It also desperately hopes that the bureaucracies of the two CGTs will manage to prevent whole workforces of employed workers being drawn into these movements. That is the rationale behind its various 'populist' promises. They are meant to create a situation in which the forces of the state can be let loose against the movement on the streets.

But it cannot fulfil these promises without upsetting the powerful financial and industrial interests. Argentinian capitalism is simply not in a situation where the government can satisfy the immediate demands of the mass of the middle classes, let alone the employed workers, without upsetting the most powerful capitalist groupings. And these groups will use every means in their power to exert pressure on it. Major sections already long for the ability to use the army as well as the police to 'restore' order across the length and breadth of the country.

They are a long way from being able to do such things at the moment. They still need a 'populist' government of the Duhalde sort, even if they moan about that government and may opt for some other figure at its head. But they will take advantage of any success Duhalde has in cooling down the mass movement to push ahead with more ambitious and more repressive schemes. They can be expected, for example, to provide encouragement to some of the right wing nationalist groups that have flourished in the past—not necessarily to bring them to power, but to use them as a force to push the political life of the country in safer, more right wing directions. They will be hoping to feed off the very bitterness created by the economic crisis. The level of unemployment, the bankruptcy of small businesses, and the atomisation and isolation produced by poverty can all open people up to lure of right wing ideas. The 1990s in Argentina did not just see the rise of the *piqueteros*—it also saw agitation against immigrants from Chile, Paraguay and Bolivia, and a swing of disaffected voters towards a far right party in some elections. As Pablo Pozzi wrote two years ago, 'Racism has increased significantly. Jokes, comments and discrimination are often directed at the recent immigrants from neighbouring countries and from South Korea. This racism is also expressed in the notions that *chilotes* (Chileans) and *boliguayos* (Bolivians and Paraguayans) are lazy, backward, thieving people who have come to steal jobs from Argentinians... Recent research demonstrates that...racism...has increased over the past decade'.[86] The upsurge of struggle has, for the moment, drowned the voices of those racist and nationalist demagogues who would try to gain politically from such sentiments. Significantly, the resolutions passed by the neighbourhood assemblies express solidarity with the immigrant groups. But there must be the danger of a renewed hearing for racists and right wing nationalists if the mass activity of the *cacerolazos* and the *piqueteros* does not succeed in dealing with the desperate poverty of half the country's population.

For this reason, it is not good enough for the left in Argentina simply to extol what has happened in the last six weeks. The lesson of the great world crisis of the 1930s is that such conditions can open the door to revolutionary hope (Spain in 1931 and 1936, France in 1934-1936) but also counter-revolutionary despair (Germany in 1933). The left has to try to carry the movement forward so that the hope prevails over the despair.

Two things are key here. There is the generalisation of the political and social demands already emerging from the popular assemblies—worksharing between the employed and unemployed without loss of pay, welfare benefits sufficient to lift people out of poverty, nationalisation of the banks, renationalisation of the privatised companies, seizure of meat and grain from the agro-commercial firms and supermarket chains to feed people.

But alongside this there have to be attempts to spread the mobilisation and the organisation so as to tap the forces capable of implementing such demands. A programme of action is no good to a hungry person so long as it is simply printed on paper—which is why scholastic disputes over the exact wording of such programmes is a diversion from the struggle. What is needed is the power to begin to implement such a programme. In Argentina, that means involving employed workers who are still under the influence of the trade union bureaucracy. Such workers are fewer in number than before the economic crisis. But there are still millions of them (1,610,000 in greater Buenos Aires, 210,000 in greater Córdoba, 110,000 in greater Rosario at the end of last year[87]) and their labour is still essential to the day to day functioning of Argentinian capitalism. Like workers elsewhere in the world, mass unemployment has created reluctance among many of them towards entering into any struggle they fear may not be won. The trade union bureaucracy has been playing on this fear, telling them that their only hope is Duhalde. But they have lived through an experience in the last six weeks unlike that anywhere else. They have seen how mass action can overthrow governments—and many of them have been involved in the mass actions of the last few weeks as individuals, even if not as organised workplace contingents. What is more, some at least have been involved in very bitter workplace struggles in these weeks to defend their jobs and have formed links with the *piqueteros*, and others cannot avoid having to fight to defend their living standards against inflation. This opens up the prospect of them being won to the far reaching demands that only they have the power to implement—demands whose implementation would carry the Argentinian uprising in a clear anti-capitalist direction.

The Argentinian left, as we have seen, is weak. But situations like that in Argentina transform the consciousness of the people by the thousand. Reading the Argentinian papers and watching the Argentinian news broadcasts on the internet remind me of the atmosphere of France in 1968 or Portugal in 1975, of radicalisation on a mass scale, but against the background of a much greater social crisis. The left in Argentina has to throw all of its relatively weak forces into action, in an effort to create a revolutionary pole of attraction in the midst of the explosive ups and downs of a whole society in economic, social and political crisis.

Meanwhile, for the left elsewhere there is a very simple lesson to be taken seriously. In the midst of a world system undergoing repeated, convulsive crisis, all that is solid can melt into air. A stable political system in which the revolutionary left seems marginalised can suddenly be twisted apart, producing great upsurges from below. The old left that became demoralised in much of the world in the late 1980s and early 1990s and the new left born since Seattle can suddenly be confronted with potentially revolutionary situations.

Argentina is not an exception. It is not some remote and foreign place. The crisis is not a result simply of the politicians adopting 'mistaken' policies. Nor is it a matter of them simply succumbing to privatisation and neo-liberalism because of their all too evident personal corruption or the all too obvious foreign pressures. Argentinian capitalism is a weak capitalism which has found no way to cope with the impact of successive world crises except to attack the conditions its workers and lower middle classes have taken for granted in the past. And that is a problem that besets many other capitalisms, including some we usually think of as strong. Argentina is not the only place in which we are going to feel the desperate need for a revolutionary party with serious roots in the working class.

**Notes**

1 Quoted in *Le Monde*, 21 January 2002.

2 R Munck with R Falcon and B Galitelli, *Argentina From Anarchism to Peronism* (London, 1987), p101.

3 For a graphic account of this period, see D James, *Resistance and Integration: Peronism and the Argentine Working Class, 1946-1976* (Cambridge, 1988), pp14-15, 25-30.

4 R Munck with R Falcon and B Galitelli, op cit, p127.

5 The relationship between Peronism and the working class was far too intricate to do sufficient justice to it in a couple of paragraphs here. For a longer, excellent, account see D James, op cit.

6 R Munck with R Falcon and B Galitelli, op cit, p144 and p163.

7 'Argentina', *Citta Futura*, anno vi, n3 (Rome, March 1974), p15.

8 Details in O Alba, '*El Cordobazo*', *Socialismo o Barbarie*, no 7, 2001.

9 R Munck with R Falcon and B Galitelli, op cit, p171.

10 For full accounts of these events, see J P Brennan, *The Labor Wars in Córdoba 1955-1976* (Harvard, 1994), and chapter 9 of D James, op cit.

11 References to Argentina as a 'semi-colony' are widespread on the Argentinian left. In some cases the phrase is meant simply as a synonym for 'impoverished'. In other cases it signifies explicitly that the local bourgeoisie lack political sovereignty because it is economically weak and therefore forced into a subordinate position in its economic relations with capitalism in richer and more powerful countries. This is to make a fundamental theoretical error. A colony

lacks political independence. Once it achieves political independence—ie to be no longer dominated militarily by some other power—it ceases to be a colony. The fact that it cannot attain some mythical economic independence from the world system is neither here nor there.

This was the point Lenin made repeatedly in his polemics against those, like Rosa Luxemburg and Nikolai Bukharin, who opposed the demand for national self determination in the years before the Russian Revolution. They claimed that there could not be economic independence and so there could not be political independence either. He was insistent one was different to the other. The term 'semi-colonial' can only be correctly ascribed to countries where direct foreign military interference makes nonsense of the pretence of political independence—for instance, countries like El Salvador, Nicaragua and Panama through much of the 20th century. It cannot be applied to a country with a ruling class which runs its own state, exercising an internal monopoly of armed power, and then does deals with the great imperialist powers in which it is a junior partner. Not to see this has led those influenced by Stalinism repeatedly to look for alliances in pursuit of 'national independence' with a local bourgeoisie that already exercises state power—this has been prevalent, for instance, in India, where it has led the Communist parties to back the military adventures by the Indian state. It can also lead even those from the Trotskyist tradition to come out with absurd formulations like speaking of the 'bourgeoisie in backward countries' (including Argentina) as 'a semi-oppressed class', of Argentina as 'a semi-colonial nation lacking sovereignty' and as only having achieved 'pseudo-industrialisation' in the period from the 1930s to the 1970s. (J Sanmartino of the Argentinian PTS, 'The Impotence of Progressivism', *International Strategy*, no 1 (May 2001), pp36, p33). One wonders what a pseudo car plant looks like! More seriously, it opens the door to trying to make political alliances with local capitalism. After all, in a real colonial situation, in the face of the occupying army of an imperialist power, we would have to provide unconditional but critical support to any struggle of the bourgeoisie to drive the occupying forces out (as we do, for instance, in the case of Palestine today).

Lenin had no doubt that Argentina was 'politically independent', even though economically 'dependent' on Britain in the years running up the First World War. In *Imperialism, the Highest Stage of Capitalism*, he states, 'Another form of dependence' to that of the 'semi-colony...is provided by Argentina', where 'the British finance capital...acquires...strong connections...with the Argentinian bourgeoisie, with the circles that that control all of that country's economic and political life' (V I Lenin, *Collected Works*, vol 22 (Moscow, 1964)). For him it matters that 'the circles' in control of the state are Argentinian and not British. It means there is no struggle to be waged by the bourgeoisie and those under its influence for the political right to self determination. Elsewhere he emphasised the point, explicitly contrasting the situation in Argentina with that in other countries which lack political independence. In these the conditions existed for a struggle for sections of the bourgeoisie and petty bourgeoisie to clash with the imperialist powers over the demand for political independence. He was insistent, however, that political independence was not the same as economic independence, which, he held, was not possible for any capitalist country involved in a world capitalist system dominated by the great firms of the imperialist powers. See 'The Nascent Trends of Imperialist Economism', 'A Reply to P Kievsky (Y Pyatakov)', and 'A Caricature of Marxism and Imperialist Economism', in V I Lenin, *Collected Works*, vol 23 (Moscow, 1964), pp13-76. The explicit reference to Argentina is on page 44. Of course, in countries where firms from the imperialist powers own banks, industries, etc there is a struggle to wage against them as well as against the local capitalists. And workers have to be prepared to find the imperialist powers assisting the local bourgeoisie in crushing resistance to anti-capitalist struggles. There is an anti-imperialist dimension to workers' struggles, but it is not at all the same as that in a colony or semi-colony, where the forces of imperialism fully or partly exercise direct political power.

12 M A García, *Peronismo: Desarrollo Economico y Lucha de Clase en Argentina* (Eplugés de Llobregat, 1980), p29. The Argentinian figure was 749, that of France 571 and that of Italy 414.

13 See the arguments against those who see Argentina as being a 'neo-colony' in A Dabat and L Lorenzano, *Conflicto Malvinense y Crisis Nacional* (Mexico, 1982), pp68-71.

14 M A García, op cit, p29.

15 Ibid, p42.

16 The figures are given in 'Argentina', *Citta Futura*, op cit.

17 See the comparison of Italian and Argentinian growth rates in M A Garcia, 'Argentina: El Veintenio Desarrollista', in *Debate*, no 4 (Rome, April-May 1978), p20.

18 'Argentina', *Citta futura*, op cit, p3.

19 Ibid, p7.

20 Figures for Argentinian wages in 1995 given in 'Expected Wages in Selected NME Countries', at http://ia.ita.doc.gov/wages/95wages/95wages.htm

21 See UNDP, *World Development Report* (Oxford, 1997).

22 Figures in R Munck with R Falcon and B Galitelli, op cit, p209.

23 E Cárpena, 'El capitalismo en Argentina', in *Debate*, op cit, p17.

24 According to R Munck with R Falcon and B Galitelli, op cit, pp208-209.

25 Federal Reserve Bank of Cleveland, *Economic Commentary*, September 1999.

26 Ibid.

27 'Prologo' to M A García, *Peronismo: Desarrollo Economico y Lucha de Clase en Argentina*, op cit, p6.

28 See the figures in *Debate*, op cit, p114.

29 According to A Dabat and L Lorenzano, op cit, p56.

30 *Business Week*, 21 October 1991.

31 *Financial Times*, 'Survey On Argentina', 19 September 1997.

32 Ibid.

33 The figures given by the US Agency for International Development, Washington DC, 1996, show a rise of about 4 percent—although this figure may be misleading since we know that in this period there was growth of low paid unregistered employment in the black economy.

34 See figure 5 in P Sanguinetti and J Pantano, *Changes in Production and Employment Structure and Relative Wages in Argentina and Uruguay*, World Bank Sponsored Paper (August, 2001).

35 Ibid, p3.

36 *Financial Times*, 'Survey On Argentina', op cit.

37 J Stiglitz, reprinted in *ATTAC Newsletter* 113, available at http://attac.org

38 According to the *Financial Times*, 9 October 2001.

39 P Sanguinetti and J Pantano, op cit.

40 Instituto Nacional de Estadística y Censos, *Republica Argentina* (available at www.indec.mecon.gov.ar).

41 *Financial Times*, 30 October 2001.

42 M Mussa, *Financial Times*, 12 November 2001.

43 According to *El País*, 21 December 2001, 42.5 percent of foreign investment is from European Union countries (more than half of this from Spain) and 37.4 percent from the US.

44 *Página 12*, web version, 25 January 2002, www.pagina12.com.ar

45 'Otra Cacerolazo Contra el Corralito', *Página 12*, web version, 11 January 2002, op cit.
46 *Página 12*, 6 January 2002.
47 F Huertas, *Libération*, 28 January 2002.
48 S Calloni, *La Jornada*, 21 January 2001.
49 E-mailed information from an Argentinian revolutionary socialist.
50 This list is taken from a single issue of the paper *Prensa Obrera*.
51 The original Trotskyist organisation was led by Nahuel Moreno.
52 J A Montes et al, *Astillero Rio Santiago* (Buenos Aires, 1999), pp54-55.
53 Quoted ibid, p66.
54 P Pozzi, 'Popular Upheaval and Capitalist Transformation in Argentina', *Latin American Perspectives*, vol 27, no 5 (September 2000), p74.
55 J A Montes et al, op cit, p105.
56 P Pozzi, op cit, p79.
57 Ibid, p83.
58 The attempts to do so in *La Verdad Obrera* (8 January 2002) and *Prensa Obrera* (28 December 2001) do not hold water. The fact that there were previous struggles does not mean there was no spontaneous movement of vast numbers of new people into action, constituting a qualitative change form what had gone before.
59 The point is well made in M Romano, 'Four General Strikes in 15 Months', in the PTS journal, *International Strategy*, no 1 (May 2001), p31.
60 As does J Petras, 'Argentina, the Big Bed and the Popular Uprising', available at www.eurosur.org/rebellion.petras.htm
61 H Camarero, P Pozzi and A Schneider, 'Unrest and Repression in Argentina', *New Politics*, vol 7, no 1 (new series), whole no 25 (Summer 1998).
62 Ibid.
63 P Pozzi, op cit, p63.
64 Details from O Alba, 'La Lucha Por el Pan', *Socialismo o Barbarie*, no 6, 2001.
65 See, for instance, the description in M Romano, 'Four General Strikes in 15 months', op cit, p27.
66 *Página 12*, 31 March 2001.
67 See, for example, the account of the killing of two civilians during the road blockade in General Mosconi, north of Salta, in *Página 12*, 1 June 2001.
68 R Saenz in *Socialismo o Barbarie*, no 6, 2001.
69 See the rather bitterly toned article by local MAS activist Laura Correale in *Socialismo o Barbarie*, no 7, 2001.
70 O Alba, 'La Lucha Por el Pan', op cit.
71 L Correale, *Socialismo o Barbarie*, op cit.
72 J Petras, op cit
73 See, for instance, 'El MAS en Argentinazo', *Socialismo o Barbarie*, no 10, January 2002. See also the bitter diatribe against Petras in *La Verdad Obrero*, 8 January 2002.
74 This is clear from the papers of the *Partido Obrero* and the *Partido de Trabajadores por el Socialism* and the magazine of the *Movemiento al Socialismo*, *Socialismo o Barbarie*.
75 P Pozzi, op cit, p81.
76 Ibid.
77 For a criticism of the CTA position, see O Alba, 'Cuadro de Situacíon', *Socialismo o Barbarie*, no 4, 2000, and R Ramirez and A Orbush, 'Triste, Soitario, Final...', *Socialismo o Barbarie*, no 2, 2000.
78 Deputy economics minister J Todesca, quoted in *La Jornada*, 8 January 2002.
79 *Financial Times*, 24 January 2002.
80 David Cufré in *Página 12*, 1 February 2002.
81 T Catán in *Financial Times*, 4 February 2002.

82 S Calloni, *La Jornada*, 8 February 2001.
83 The phrase is used by A Zalat in *Página 12*, 4 February 2002.
84 According to A Zalat, ibid.
85 According to A Zalat, ibid. See also the analysis of M Itzcovich in *Il Manifesto*, 5 February 2002.
86 P Pozzi, op cit, p76.
87 Figures given in *Página 12*, 22 January 2002, are for the number employed in workplaces of more than 12 employees. They show a loss of 122,000 jobs in these cities in the year.

# The return of the rank and file?

MARTIN SMITH

The problems facing the trade union movement in Britain today are all too obvious. After all, for the past 20 years, politicians and many academics have been more than keen to declare the working class dead. But it is becoming increasingly clear that small victories, compounded bitterness and the explosion of political struggles, like the anti-capitalist movement, are giving confidence to trade unionists.

Trade union militancy can revive from periods of defeat in many ways. The most obvious is a major strike victory, which in turn can inspire other workers to fight. Alternatively it can come about through the rising of general political consciousness. Today the latter appears to be the case. The political recovery of the left seems to be inspiring a revival in trade union confidence.

For 20 years socialists and working class activists in Britain have seen the trade union movement in retreat. Last summer there were signs that a revolt was fermenting against New Labour's privatisation plans. The TUC conference in September was billed as the big showdown between the unions and Blair. But the attack on the World Trade Centre derailed that confrontation. The TUC conference was closed early and the battle was postponed. The TUC and some union leaders cynically used the tragedy to put the brakes on the fight against privatisation. For instance, the GMB union dropped its £1 million advertising campaign against privatisation and in effect the CWU signed a three-month no-strike deal with Consignia. While the union leaders backed off, the employers used this 'new-found solidarity' to announce massive job cuts.

But three months later the revival looks like it is back on course—a fierce strike by guards and station staff on South West Trains sparked off a wave of disputes right across the rail industry and beyond. These strikes created a massive political crisis for New Labour. Tony Blair's 'wreckers' speech at Labour's spring conference left hundreds of thousands of trade unionists livid. It also forced John Monks, general secretary of the TUC, to come out and attack New Labour. More importantly, renationalisation of the rail industry is back on the agenda and a debate is opening up around the question of the funding of public services like the NHS and education.

I want to look at three key issues. What factors have created this new militancy in Britain? What are the hurdles facing the revival of this working class militancy, and what forms of organisation are trade union activists creating in order to overcome the very real problems they confront?

**The anti-capitalist movement**

Every major union, with the exception of the AEEU, has expressed some support for the anti-capitalist movement. British trade union branches have sent respectably sized delegations to anti-capitalist demonstrations in Nice, Genoa and Brussels. More importantly, the fighting spirit of anti-capitalism has permeated into the ranks of the movement. Two examples will suffice. At a South West Train strikers' meeting, rank and file activists called on union leaders to contact the anti-capitalist movement to see if they could organise a mass demonstration outside Waterloo.[1] Workers themselves may not be confident to blockade their depots and stations but they like the idea of someone else doing it. Secondly, the editorial board of the rank and file paper *Post Worker* were surprised to discover that they received more letters about the anti-capitalist movement than they did about any other issue including privatisation, job cuts and pay.[2]

The anti-capitalist movement has created a high degree of politicisation inside the unions. The ideas of the anti-capitalist movement are widely circulated. Billy Hayes, general secretary of the CWU, has recommended to his members that they read George Monbiot's anti-capitalist book *Captive State: The Corporate Takeover of Britain*. The struggles of Latino workers in the US have prompted the TUC and the TGWU to set up union groups for low paid foreign workers. They have adopted some of the methods employed in the US—film shows, dances and cultural evenings—to recruit to the unions.[3] One final example comes from the TSSA (the union for clerical and technical grades on the railway). Two years ago delegates at the union conference were discussing the fascinating problem of train delays caused by 'leaves on the line'. The executive's solution was to call for the cutting down of all trees and bushes along every railway embankment. One delegate opposed the executive's proposals claiming that to do this would not only damage the environment, but would encourage the deforestation of the Brazilian rainforests by multinational corporations. The top table told the delegate that the union had to promote policies that were realistic and that the delegate was 'not living in the real world'. The conference rejected the executive's proposal unanimously![4]

The anti-capitalist struggle is giving nourishment to the trade union movement around the world. In the last few years, trade unionists have responded to globalisation and its impact with general or mass political strikes. In Argentina, India, Spain, Bolivia, South Africa and France, union federations have called on their members to challenge privatisation, austerity measures, job cuts and other symptoms of increased corporate power.

The anti-capitalist movement has brought energy and excitement to the left. Its ability to politically generalise means that a layer of workers are also making the connections between privatisation, globalisation and the need for resistance.

## New Labour

The anti-capitalist, anti-privatisation mood is now so widely diffused among workers that it is opening up a gap between many of them and the leaders of the Labour Party.

When New Labour won its historic general election landslide victory in 1997 it promised to take the rail back into public ownership, fund public services and end sleaze. Its failure to do so has created massive bitterness. Under intense pressure from their members, union leaders are heading towards a showdown with Blair over privatisation. John Edmonds, the GMB's general secretary, gave vent to his members' feelings when he warned the government at a fringe meeting at the Labour Party's spring conference, 'Our polls show only 11 percent support for privatisation. The poll tax at its highest had 14 percent—and as far as I can remember the poll tax wasn't exactly a great electoral success… The government has created—totally unnecessarily—its own poll tax, its own imploding policy that is going to drag it down'.[5] Until recently the GMB has been seen as an ultra-loyal supporter of the Labour Party.

The debate with Labour is also opening up in more unexpected ways. For the past 100 years the trade union movement has been the backbone, both politically and financially, of the Labour Party. That support is beginning to crack. Two years ago at the CWU's annual conference delegates voted to 'break all links, both politically and financially, with the Labour Party if it went ahead with the privatisation of the Post Office'. At last year's firefighters' annual conference delegates voted to open up their political fund to other parties, and in UNISON, Britain's biggest public sector union, conference delegates voted to conduct a review of the political fund. At the beginning of the year the GMB announced it was going to reduce its contribution to the Labour Party by £2 million over four years and will not support candidates who support the Private Finance Initiative. As Labour continues with its anti working class measures and privatisation plans, this bitterness can only get deeper.

The Labour Party relies on the trade union bureaucracy to control the rank and file and act as fully as possible in the interest of the Labour Party. A sign of the weakening of Labour's hold over the trade union movement has been the growth of the Scottish Socialist Party and the Socialist Alliance. They have both attracted a small but significant number of trade union militants into their ranks. Mark Serwotka (PCS general secretary elect) is a member of the Socialist Alliance, and Bob Crow (RMT assistant secretary) has spoken on Socialist Alliance platforms. This is something the mainstream press has been more than happy to publicise recently.

Trade union leaders and for the most part trade union members accept there is a division between politics and economics. Put simply, trade unions deal with wages and conditions, and politicians deal with the economy and the state. Accepting this blunts the ability of workers to fight back. Any move towards clearly linking politics and economics makes the recovery of the trade union movement far more effective. A significant upturn in class struggle could make things very difficult for Blair.

## The war in Afghanistan

The scale of the opposition to Bush's so called 'war against terrorism' has been considerable in Britain. Trade unions played a small but significant role in this movement. Within three months of 11 September four major trade unions—ASLEF, CWU, RMT and TSSA—had come out against the war. Several other unions called for a cessation in the bombing. Trade unionists joined the anti-war marches in significant numbers. There were over 80 union banners on the second national demonstration against the war in Afghanistan. As journalist John Pilger noted, 'We have not seen opposition by trade unionists against a war on this scale since the Vietnam War'.[6] According to the Stop the War Coalition over 500 union branches have passed anti-war motions.

The political radicalisation produced by the anti-war movement has been duplicated on a smaller scale in other campaigns—defending council housing, stopping the rise of the Nazis and numerous local issues. The attacks by New Labour, and the inspiration of the anti-capitalist movement and the anti-war movement are forcing trade union activists to generalise politically.

## The slow recovery

The massive gap between the political anger in Britain and the level of class struggle cannot be sustained. Trade union militancy will either have to rise to the level of the political movement or the political movement will fall back to the level of the class struggle. At the moment trade union confidence is being strengthened by the impetus from outside events.

The fall in trade union membership appears to be bottoming out—in fact it is once again on the increase. According to the Certification Officer, there are now 7.9 million trade union members in Britain, an increase of 46,000 on the previous year.[7] Last year was the second successive year in which membership increased. More interestingly, some of the unions with the biggest number of recruits are the CWU and PCS. Both unions have played a key role in the recent strikes. The proportion of workers who belong to a union (union density) remains steady at around 30 percent.[8] Once again trade unions are popular. A TUC survey conducted in 1999 found that three out of five workers not in a union would like to join one.[9]

It is important to remember that the recent period has not been the first time trade unionism in Britain has suffered a major setback in support. For example, union membership almost halved during the economic slump of 1880 and did not recover until the emergence of the mass strikes that developed during the New Unionism of 1889. Also, in the aftermath of the1926 General Strike trade union membership collapsed from its height of 6.5 million in 1920 to 3.6 million in 1929.[10] But each slump has been followed by a revival in trade union membership and confidence.

Despite its weaknesses, New Labour's Employment Relations Act has resulted in an increase in the number of union recognition deals. A survey conducted by the TUC found that there were 470 new recognition agreements last year, almost three times the number signed the previous year. As a result over 120,000 more workers are now covered by a recognised trade union.[11] Union recognition deals are at present outstripping the growth of union membership. If activists and trade union officials use the deals to recruit on the shop floor membership can soon start to flourish—this is already happening in a number of industries. Of course, there are weaknesses—some of the deals signed are single-union 'sweetheart deals'—but any growth in union recruitment will give confidence to activists on the shop floor.

Low unemployment levels have given workers confidence to use their collective strength. A skills shortage in the job market has seen workers 'flexing their muscles' in the privatised utilities—gas, water, electricity and more obviously the rail.

Rail privatisation has been a disaster for the workforce. Jobs have been shed on a massive scale and working conditions have been attacked. But there is another side to this story. The greed of the privatised rail companies meant that they have cut corners, laid off qualified drivers and cut back on research and development programmes—all for a quick buck. When demand for rail travel increased, the rail companies were chronically short of qualified drivers. A poaching war ensued. The drivers' union, ASLEF, was quick to exploit this. Drivers on ScotRail recently demonstrated just how vulnerable the rail companies are when they organised an overtime ban and refused to work on their rest days. One in four trains did not run. Over the last few years drivers' wages have been continually leap-frogging one another. Rail workers employed on other grades have refused to sit idly by and watch the wage gap get wider and wider. They too are now striking for better wages and conditions.

Another indicator of the growing radicalisation taking place in the trade union movement is the recent election victories of left wing union activists. In the last four years we have seen Mick Rix (an ex-member of Arthur Scargill's Socialist Labour Party) elected as general secretary of ASLEF. Billy Hayes is now general secretary of the CWU, Mark Serwotka (who describes himself as a revolutionary socialist) has been elected as general secretary of the PCS, and Bob Crow has been elected as general secretary of the RMT by a massive majority.

For socialists these results are an important indicator of the mood on the shop floor. Workers in these unions have voted for candidates who have opposed privatisation and partnership and have supported their members on strike. These election results have clearly shocked New Labour. The *Financial Times* reports:

> *Another minister with union ties says that traditional methods of influencing unions do not work with the new generation of leaders. These people are not interested in the Labour Party. They are not interested in making deals to make life easier for Labour in power and they certainly would not be impressed by an invitation to Number Ten for dinner. They want an old fashioned trial of strength with the company.*[12]

New Labour will be keeping a close eye on the leadership elections taking place in the GMB and the TGWU over the next 18 months.

If we look below the level of the unions' structure to the actual balance of class forces in industrial struggles the picture is more uneven. The British trade union movement found itself in a transitory period during the 1990s. Still reeling from the defeats of the 1980s, it began to regain its confidence bit by bit. This painfully slow process was already beginning to be observed in a number of disputes such as the Timex strike of 1994 and the signal workers' dispute of the same year. Things now appear to be speeding up. A brief look at some of the key disputes over the past five years gives some sense of the scale of the recovery and the problems the working class still has to overcome.

*British Airways:* Cabin crew staff employed by British Airways were the first major group of workers to take industrial action under the New Labour government. Workers voted to hold a 72-hour strike in opposition to cutbacks in July 1997. In the run up to the action staff came under massive pressure. Bosses threatened to sack every striker, sue them and even sent managers round to their homes to intimidate them. In the end 1,600 cabin staff went sick. The mass stayaway cost British Airways £125 million. Eventually BASSA officials accepted a poor deal.[13]

*Jubilee Line:* The Jubilee Line extension was the biggest building project in London between 1995 and 1997. A series of unofficial stoppages over wages and conditions created a very strong independent union organisation. The Jubilee Line electricians became the catalysts for a new rank and file movement amongst electricians belonging to the AEEU in the construction industry. In October 1997 management announced that they were going to downgrade electricians' work. AEEU branches demanded that their union organised a national strike. Their pleas were ignored. The Jubilee Line electricians called a one-day unofficial strike. Around 5,000 struck in London, Glasgow, Newcastle and Kent. Around 300 electricians held an unofficial march on Downing Street. A second unofficial strike was held, and over 30 sites walked out involving up to 9,000 workers. This time 1,000 strikers laid siege to their union headquarters. Eventually union officials were able to win a vote to accept the regrading, but only by using the most outrageous tactics. Leading militants were expelled from the union and ballot papers were sent to groups of workers who were not involved in the regrading. However, the rank and file activity paid dividends for the electricians. When they started working on the Jubilee Line extension they were the lowest paid electricians in London. By the end of the job their wages were the highest in the country.[14]

*The car industry:* When BMW announced its plans in April 2000 to shut its Longbridge plant with the loss of 12,000 jobs, anger swept across the West Midlands. A powerful publicity campaign followed by a 100,000-strong demonstration put pressure on the government to come up with a rescue package and a new buyer. To this day Longbridge remains open and over 6,000 workers still have their jobs. Later in the year Vauxhall in Luton announced that it was going to close its plant with the loss of 2000 jobs. Workers laid siege to the manager's offices and riot police had to be called. An unofficial strike and a 20,000-strong demo ensured that several thousand workers kept their jobs.[15]

*NHS:* Health workers in the Dudley group of hospitals held a series of strikes against the transfer of NHS buildings and 600 jobs to the private sector. The strikers held out for ten months and only ended their action when the PFI scheme was finally signed. As well as organising a 200-strong conference to discuss privatisation, the strikers also launched their own rank and file paper. Even more remarkably the health workers put forward a striker as a Socialist Alliance candidate in the general election.[16]

*London Underground:* In the run-up to last year's general election members of ASLEF and the RMT voted overwhelmingly to strike over the question of safety on the tube. But the real issue behind the strike was opposition to New Labour's privatisation plans for London Underground. Terrified of united action, management went to the courts and got an injunction served on the RMT, thus making their strike illegal. The anger among members of both unions was palpable. Unofficial meetings were held and members of the RMT decided to break the law and support their colleagues in ASLEF. The strike was magnificent—95 percent of trains did not run. The RMT once again re-balloted and won a strike vote. New Labour manoeuvred to get the strikes called off. A series of meetings were held between ASLEF, the government, Ken Livingstone and the TUC. The ASLEF executive buckled and called its strike off, leaving the RMT to fight alone. This time rank and file ASLEF activists ensured their members did not cross RMT picket lines. Sadly the RMT then decided that it would not call any further action.[17]

*The post:* Over 50,000 post workers took illegal, unofficial strike action last May. The strike began when post workers in Liverpool and Stockport refused to handle work from Watford sorting office, where workers were on strike. The strike soon spread to Preston, Manchester, North Wales, Chester, Maidstone, Dartford, Newcastle and all of London. Mass pickets were organised at the Liverpool, Cardiff and Watford offices. The strike lasted almost a week and only ended when management completely capitulated. One activist claimed after the strike, 'Using direct and militant tactics we achieved far more than months or years of negotiations'.[18]

Many of these strikes contained elements of the past—lack of rank and file confidence, reliance on trade union leaders. But in many cases they also displayed a new confidence to act independently of the officials, to break the law and to use militant tactics. One more very important attribute marks out all these disputes—the strikers won, or at worst the disputes ended in a partial victory. Today the defeats of the 1980s mean less to a new young layer of reps and shop stewards. 'Don't strike—look what happened to the miners' was a common refrain a decade ago. Now it is rarely, if ever, mentioned.

The pattern of industrial disputes over the past five years has been one of an explosion of anger, which in some cases—Rover and the strikes on the tube—have begun to generalise only to then fall back, usually with the help of the trade union bureaucracy. But now the number of strikes seems to be multiplying. At the time of writing disputes under way included: official action by ASLEF members on ScotRail, leading to the cancellation of one in four trains; two-day strikes by guards belonging to the RMT on Arriva Northern and four other strike ballots taking place on the rail and the tube; over 40,000 civil servants struck for two days over the removal of security screens; 150,000 postal workers voted overwhelmingly to strike over pay; 85,000 UNISON members in local government are involved in an indicative ballot over pay; and teachers in London are planning to hold a strike ballot over the question of London weighting.

Not surprisingly, the media is full of talk about a return to the 1970s and the Winter of Discontent. One right wing commentator in the *Daily Mail* noted, 'Socialism was meant to have been consigned to the dustbin of history... Yet today in Britain the far left is on the march again'.[19]

There is no doubt that New Labour fears these strikes and the dragons that they might unleash. The *Financial Times* reports, 'Privately, ministers admitted they were alarmed at the prospect of a national strike coming on top of the rail strikes which have crippled commuter services in the south and north'.[20] New Labour is terrified that further strikes could inspire a wider revolt against low pay, privatisation and the anti trade union laws.

Talk of a return to 1970s levels of industrial action is a considerable exaggeration. Nevertheless, the stakes are high. Again the *Financial Times* reports that 'unrest is not confined to the railways and has been simmering away since the general election. If the RMT wins, sparking more disputes, the "partnership" ethos that has characterised unions' broader dealings with employers under Labour could crack'.[21] The government and the employers are taking a very hard line with the strikes. Ministers are refusing to hold any meaningful negotiations with the PCS, the civil servants' union, and they are giving tacit support to Brian Souter's union-busting operation on SWT. The outcome of these disputes is far from certain, but one thing is clear—the government's stance is having the effect of straining relations with the union movement even further.

Documents written and compiled by Mike Power, an official at the TUC, have been leaked and published in *Socialist Worker*. They clearly demonstrate that the TUC and the right wing of the union movement are getting organised and are trying to block the left. The documents also reveal that a senior Labour minister met with senior officials of the TUC to explain why they could not give an inch to unions like the CWU, PCS and the RMT for fear of 'unleashing a dragon'.[22]

Underlying the intervention of both TUC and Labour leaders is that they rightly believe they are losing their grip over a significant part of the Labour movement.

## The 1950s to today

'The tradition of all the dead generations weighs like a nightmare on the brain of the living,' wrote Karl Marx.[23] In order to understand the problems any re-emerging rank and file revolt faces, it is important to take a very brief look at the development of the trade union movement over the past 50 years.

Trade unionism grew steadily during the long economic boom of the 1950s and 1960s. Not only did union membership continue to grow in the traditional heartlands, but recruitment also exploded in white-collar unions based in education, local government and the civil service.[24] The shop stewards committees led the fight in the workplace to win better pay and conditions. The Communist Party (CP) had the ability at that time to move the shop stewards movement as a whole despite the fact that only a tiny percentage of shop stewards were members. The gains workers made came about through their own self activity and not through their leaders. This struggle to win improvements in wages and conditions has been called 'do it yourself reformism'.

However, by the late 1960s and early 1970s the long boom came to an end and the first major economic crisis rocked the Western economies. The combination of an economic crisis and an anti-union offensive led to a series of clashes with the bosses and the Tory government. A strike by the miners for better pay in 1972 forced the government to make a humiliating climbdown. This was followed by strikes on the railways and in engineering. In the same year five dockers were imprisoned in

Pentonville prison for breaking the anti-union laws. Tens of thousands of workers struck demanding their release. The pressure was so great that the TUC was forced to call a general strike. Before it could be acted on, the Official Solicitor secured a quick release of the dockers. This was a truly amazing victory for the working class. A further strike by the miners in 1974 finished off the Heath government.

One historian, Royden Harrison, called the struggle during the Heath government 'the most extraordinary triumph of trade unionism in its long conflict with the government. The labour unrest of 1970-1974 was far more massive and incomparably more successful than its predecessors of 1910 and 1919... First they blew the government "off course"; then landed it on the rocks... Nothing like this had ever been seen before!'[25]

Once again it was the shop stewards movement that led these struggles. But as Tony Cliff and Donny Gluckstein explained, the CP's role was far from glorious:

> *Its leadership...had long abandoned revolutionary socialism for a policy of changing society through achieving a majority of left Labour and Communist MPs. This logic had not yet nullified the membership's fighting ability, but it sapped it inexorably. Because the Communist Party's politics were stifling the ability of its rank and file militants to lead, a space developed for small groups like the International Socialists (the forerunner of the SWP) to develop a fledgling rank and file movement.*[26]

When Labour took office in 1974 it ditched its radical promises and set about introducing spending cuts. However, the key demand from international capital, big business and the city was for a reduction in workers' wages. What the Tories failed to do by force, Labour achieved with the help of the trade union bureaucracy. Labour introduced the now infamous Social Contract. Union leaders talked about the 'national interest' and the result was a fall in workers' living standards. The shop stewards movement was still dominated by the politics of the Labour Party and the Communist Party. It was one thing to strike against the Tories, but large sections of the shop stewards movement shied away from fighting their 'own government'. They, along with the trade union bureaucracy, sold Labour's incomes policy to their union members. When, in late 1978, the government tried to impose a fourth wage limit, the floodgates broke. The result was the 'Winter of Discontent'. It was not part of a new rising tide of militancy, but an explosion of bitterness and demoralisation which led to the victory of Margaret Thatcher in 1979.

The aim of the Tory government was clear: it wanted to reverse the defeats the ruling class had suffered at the hands of the working class in the early 1970s. In 1978, when the Tories were still in opposition, they worked out a strategy to take the unions on. It was known as the Ridley Plan—named after the Conservative minister Nicholas Ridley. The idea was to take on the trade unions one at a time. This led to a series of confrontations, starting with the steel workers in 1980, the health workers in 1982 and the miners in 1984-1985. This was closely followed by the print workers' dispute at Wapping and finally confrontations with the seafarers and the dockers. The Tories won every battle. No other European working class movement went through such a heavy series of defeats.

It is clear to any trade union activist today that the movement paid a heavy price. The balance of class forces not only shifted from labour to capital but from the rank and file to the trade union bureaucracy. The TUC and trade union leaders talked less and less in terms of class conflict and more and more in favour of partnership with the bosses. Workers' confidence to fight took a massive dive. The number of strikes fell and remained incredibly low throughout most of the 1990s.

These defeats also took their toll on the shop stewards and the union reps. The legacy of those defeats is still with us today. For one thing, the lack of confidence in their members' ability to fight has made shop stewards and union reps more reliant on their union officials and less confident to call action. In a number of disputes, most notably Ford's and Peugeot, many of the stewards have been to the right of their members and in some cases have hindered action that has taken place.

For example, car workers at the Peugeot plant in Coventry rejected several pay offers made by the company during the summer of 2000. On each occasion the shop stewards committee recommended acceptance. In the run up to the strike the stewards did everything they could to undermine the action. However, when the 24-hour strike took place it was absolutely solid. Even then shop stewards refused to bring strike placards, armbands or the union banner to the picket line. Only one or two union reps joined the picket lines. It was left to rank and file activists to carry the strike!

But it is important to stress that union reps have held their organisations together under the most difficult of circumstances. In a number of industries the confidence of the union reps is slowly returning. As John Rees noted in this journal recently:

> *Despite this shocking series of defeats in the 1980s the British trade union movement remained remarkably resilient. At its height union membership stood at 12 million; the number is now 8 million. But the decline was mostly a result of high unemployment, peaking at over 3 million during the 1980s, and the changing structure of industry. The government's own* **Social Trends** *survey reports that since its peak in 1979 'the largest fall in union member-*

> *ship occurred in 1992, a period of substantial job losses, and the unions have failed to recover membership loss as employment growth has recovered'.*[27]

A CWU official at a regional meeting said recently, 'The problem I face is not getting the members out, the problem is holding them back.' For many activists that comment will sound all too familiar. A brief glance at any labour history book will demonstrate that the one key factor in holding back the level of class struggle has been the trade union officials. That continues to be the case today. So what attitude should socialists take to the trade union bureaucracy?

## Trade union bureaucracy

Nearly 8 million workers belong to trade unions. They remain the best defence mechanism for working class people. For socialists they are also important for another reason. In 1844 Frederick Engels wrote that strikes 'are the military school of the working men in which they prepare themselves for the great struggles which cannot be avoided…and as schools of war the unions are unexcelled'.[28] For these reasons every socialist should join and campaign inside their union. The bosses are always the enemy but when it comes to settling scores with them the biggest hurdle workers have to overcome is often the trade union bureaucracy.

Under a democratic capitalist society the formation of a trade union bureaucracy is inherent in the very nature of trade unionism. Tony Cliff describes the trade union bureaucracy as a:

> *…distinct, basically conservative, social formation. Like the God Janus it presents two faces: it balances between the employers and the workers. It holds back and controls workers' struggles, but it has a vital interest not to push the collaboration with the employers to a point where it makes the unions completely impotent. For the official is not an independent arbitrator. If the union fails entirely to articulate members' grievances, this will lead eventually either to effective internal challenges to the leadership, or to membership apathy and organisational disintegration, with members moving to a rival union. If the bureaucracy strays too far into the bourgeois camp it will lose its base. The bureaucracy has an interest in preserving the union organisation which is the source of their income and their social status.*[29]

Put simply the trade union bureaucracy balances between the two main classes in capitalist society—the employers and the workers. Trade union officials are neither employers nor workers. A union official may employ a large number of people, but unlike a capitalist employer, this is not where a union official gains their economic or social status from. On the other hand, the union official does not suffer like the mass of workers from low wages, bullying employers or job insecurity.

How far trade union leaders' lifestyles are removed from their members' is graphically demonstrated when you look at their salaries. For example, Sir Ken Jackson, leader of the AEEU (now AMICUS), earned (if that is the right word) £90,000 last year. That astronomical amount does not include his pension contribution, expenses or perks—like his free car. One AEEU official told me that he believes Ken Jackson's annual income was closer to £130,000 a year. But it is not just Ken Jackson. NUT leader Doug McAvoy's salary was £87,576 last year, while Dave Prentis of UNISON was the poor relation, taking home just £71,969. Even Billy Hayes, the left wing leader of the CWU, takes home £71,143 before expenses![30] The average post worker takes home around £200 for a six-day week and a 5.30am start.[31]

But precisely because union leaders' power and prestige comes from their ability to defend their members and maintain their base, even the most right wing general secretary can be forced to lead a strike. Take, for example, Sir Ken Jackson. During the SWT dispute Ken Jackson openly condemned the strikers in the media. What he failed to mention was that at the same time as RMT members were striking for better pay, Amicus was balloting its members in SWT over the same issue! A union official may despise the idea of striking, they may even oppose striking, but under certain circumstances even the most reactionary union leader can be forced to fight. For if they do not they may no longer have a base.

That said, trade union leaders can only be pushed so far. They are committed to the reform of capitalism, not its overthrow. During key events in labour history—1919, 1926 and the Great Miners' Strike of 1984-1985—the trade union bureaucracy has come down on the side of the state.

Two other factors keep trade union leaders in check. Firstly, the union's machine—the headquarters, finances and organisation. The Tory anti-union laws struck the trade union leaders' Achilles' heel. The fear that during unofficial strikes the courts could sequestrate the union's funds has meant that unions have shied away from leading the kind of militant fights that can win. In effect the union machine becomes more important than the members—it becomes an end in itself.

The final factor is the link between the trade unions and the Labour Party. At times there can be strains and tensions between the two, but the fact remains that the majority of unions remain tied to Labour. That link has been weakened, but it would be a mistake to underestimate the level of influence the trade union movement still holds. Last year unions donated £15 million to the Labour Party. Just as importantly, they still wield 50 percent of votes cast at the party's annual conference. There is a positive element to this link. It means that, in however a distorted fashion, Labour still has some link to the organised working class. But that link has also meant that trade unions have often refused to call action that might damage Labour's electoral prospects.

All this said, socialists do not take a neutral position when it comes to the election of left and right union officials. Socialist should always support and campaign in elections for left wing officials in union elections. The victory of a left wing official is an indicator that members want a more confrontational union. It can also strengthen the confidence of rank and file activists to fight. The year before Mark Serwotka was elected general secretary of the PCS, the union's national disputes committee received 46 requests for industrial action ballots. In the nine months after Mark Serwotka's victory there were 175 requests for action![32]

At the same time it is important not to sow illusions in trade union officials, especially those on the left.

A J Cook is a name to evoke powerful memories. He is remembered as the man who led the miners during their bitter struggles in the 1920s, culminating in the terrible defeat of the 1926 General Strike. The Russian revolutionary Leon Trotsky wrote a series of brilliant polemics about Britain in the 1920s. In them he exposes the weakness of the left trade union officials. He made absolutely no concessions to any of the left trade union leaders, even Cook, who was the most radical of all union leaders. Trotsky always mentioned Cook in the same breath as Hicks, Purcell and the other left union officials at the time. For example, Trotsky wrote:

> *Both the rights and the lefts, including of course both Purcell and Cook, fear the utmost the beginning of the denouement. Even when they in words admit the inevitability of struggle and revolution, they are hoping in their hearts for some miracle that will release them from these perspectives. And in any event they themselves will stall, evade, temporise, shift responsibility and effectively assist Thomas* [the right wing leader of the rail workers] *over any really major question of the British labour movement.*[33]

Leon Trotsky was absolutely right. A J Cook was a prisoner of the bureaucracy. At no point during the strike did he go over the heads of the TUC and call on workers to defy their own union officials. He was trapped in his own bureaucratic straitjacket.

Last year's tube strike is a more recent example of how respected left wing officials bend under the pressure. Mick Rix, the general secretary of ASLEF, is a prominent opponent of the Tory anti trade union laws. Last year his union organised a strike for improved safety on London Underground. Yet the slightest threat from the courts that they would sequestrate the unions funds and just a little pressure from Labour ministers and TUC officials meant that he called off the strike. This was despite the fact that the overwhelming majority of his members wanted to take action and did so unofficially. Despite his left wing credentials Mick Rix is a product of his social position in society. His members on the other hand—many of whom do not regard themselves as political—were prepared to strike unofficially precisely because they had nothing to lose in breaking the law.

The real divide in the union movement is between the rank and file and trade union leaders. Socialists' attitude to all union officials should follow the argument put forward by the Clyde Workers' Committee in November 1915: 'We will support the officials just so long as they rightly represent the workers, but we will act immediately they misrepresent them'.[34] Leon Trotsky made the same point when he said, 'With the masses—always; with the vacillating leaders—sometimes, but only as long as they stand at the head of the masses'.[35]

It is the rank and file and their methods of attempting to overcome the dead weight of the trade union bureaucracy that I want to look at next.

## The Broad Left

What do you do when you have an official who sells you out? The most obvious answer is to replace them with someone new. In a number of unions—PCS, UNISON, NUT and the telecom side of the CWU—there exist organisations based on the concept of Broad Lefts. The idea behind them is to bring union activists together to challenge their old moribund leaderships and replace them with left wing officials. Several of them are experiencing a revival at the moment. For example Left Unity, the Broad Left of the PCS, has doubled its membership in the last year from around 350 to 700.[36] United Left, the Broad Left of UNISON, has seen its membership rise from 350 to around 500 over the same period.[37] The growth is a symptom of the growing impatience with the trade union bureaucracy and is also a sign that workers are attempting to find an organisational solution to their problems.

But the track record of the Broad Left is not a good one. The most established Broad Left can be found in the CWU. Its membership is almost exclusively confined to the telecom side, a legacy of the days when there was a separate telecommunications union. The CWU Broad Left has been fantastically successful in winning elections. Every single member of the Telecom national executive committee is a member of the Broad Left. The CWU's general secretary, Billy Hayes, is a supporter of the Broad Left and regularly attends meetings. The Broad Left is in a position to make a real difference. While it has controlled the NEC, BT has shed over 100,000 jobs. The left-run executive has not issued one single ballot for strike action.

This problem is not just confined to Broad Lefts today. During the 1970s the Communist Party controlled a number of Broad Lefts. Ralph Darlington takes up the problems they faced:

> *The primary importance was attached to trying to replace right wing full time trade union officials by the election of left wing officials, notably by supporting such figures as Hugh Scanlon in the AUEW* [the electricians' union] *and Jack Jones in the TGWU. But the price of this electoral strategy was the CP's growing reluctance to clash with left wing officials. The contradiction between trying to give a lead to independent rank and file militancy and trying to cultivate influence among left wing officials became increasingly apparent during the 1970s wave of industrial unrest, with the CP increasingly subordinating the former in favour of the latter.*[38]

The fundamental weakness of the Broad Left strategy is the belief that by the left capturing officer posts unions can be transformed into fighting units. The entire history of the union movement has been one of left wing union officials winning union positions, only to pursue the same line as their right wing counterparts at key moments. For example, during the 1926 General Strike left union officials Alonzo Swales, A Purcell and George Hicks agreed, along with the right wing officials, to call the strike off, leaving the miners to fight alone for the next six months. More recently, it wasn't the right wing union leaders who sold the Social Contract to the workers—it was Jack Jones of the TGWU and Hugh Scanlon—the so called 'terrible twins'.

It is not a question of the individual psychology of the left wing officials who stand for such positions, but the very nature of the job. If activists are not careful, the winning of elections can become counterposed to the fight on the shop floor. In the end, holding on to positions becomes more important than anything else. The miners won their greatest victories under right wing union president Joe Gormley, and suffered their greatest defeats under Arthur Scargill. The key to victory was not who ran the union but the confidence of the rank and file.

So what attitude should revolutionary socialists take to these movements? This is a tactical question. In unions where there are already organised Broad Lefts, socialists should join them and encourage their workmates to do the same. Socialists should also play an active role inside Broad Lefts. It is important to attend meetings, get involved in campaigning for left wing union officials and use them to build up the combativity of the rank and file. But socialists should not be uncritical of the Broad Left strategy. They should actively shape the Broad Lefts and argue for a rank and file perspective. They should encourage Broad Lefts to take a lead in supporting strikes and relating to the anger on the shop floor.

But there is another way to organise. In unions like the CWU and the RMT the embryos of a rank and file movement are emerging.

## The rank and file strategy

Rank and file organisations differ from official union structures and Broad Lefts in a number of important ways. Firstly they are organisations based around workplace delegates who are subject to account by the workers they represent. Secondly they are not based in an area or region, but located in the workplace where workers are at their strongest. Lastly they cut across the sectional divisions found inside the workplace.

Rank and file movements are not alternative unions, they are bodies which organise inside the union on the shop floor. It is worth repeating, in full, the slogan of the Clyde Workers' Committee:

> *We will support the officials just so long as they rightly represent the workers, but we will act immediately they misrepresent them. Being composed of delegates from every shop and untrammelled by obsolete rule or law, we claim to represent the true feelings of the workers. We can act immediately according to the merits of the case and the desire of the rank and file.*

A rank and file movement is not based on damning all officials or having nothing to do with trade union leaders—it is for the promotion of shop floor organisation so that it is prepared to counter a betrayal by union officials. It is also worth noting that at the heart of every rank and file organisation, revolutionary socialists have played a pivotal role. One accusation levelled at those who argue for a rank and file strategy is that they abstain from standing in union elections. This is untrue—rank and file movements have on many occasions stood for full time union positions. In the 1970s rank and file candidates stood for positions in many unions including NUPE (the manual council workers' union), ATTI (a teaching union) and the TGWU. First and foremost, a rank and file electoral challenge is not a matter of promoting an individual to change the union from the top. Instead it has to be part of a strategy to encourage and promote working class self activity. If elected, a rank and file trade union official would be expected to take home the average wage of the workers he or she represented and would be accountable to the members.

Before I move on to look at the revival of rank and file movements today, I want to look at some of the key movements of the past. History never repeats itself exactly, but these unofficial rank and file movements are still relevant today, for they are among the few models we have of a serious alternative to the rule of the trade union officials.

## The Clydeside shop stewards committee

Between 1910 and 1914 a huge wave of industrial militancy swept Britain. It became known as the Great Unrest. Bitter, mainly unofficial strikes shut down the pits in South Wales in 1910-1911. In the summer of 1911 there were violent strikes involving dockers and seafarers and the first national rail strike. There were over 10 million strike days a year and union membership doubled.[39]

The outbreak of the First World War put a temporary halt to this militancy. Union leaders urged their members to accept speed-ups and 'dilution'—the introduction of unskilled workers to the jobs previously done by craftsmen to help the war effort. This was fiercely resisted. Engineers produced vital munitions, which gave them real bargaining power. A militant rank and file movement rose amongst engineers on the Clyde and in Sheffield. This movement brought together shop floor representatives from different unions and workplaces to co-ordinate their struggles. Regular workplace bulletins and meetings kept members informed and prepared the ground for a number of skirmishes with the employers.

At its height this unofficial rank and file movement was able to launch major strikes against dilution, the largest of which involved 200,000 engineers working in 48 towns in 1917. The wartime shop stewards movement was an important step forward for the working class. It was the first independent rank and file movement in Britain. After the Russian Revolution of 1917 shop stewards began to see the rank and file committees as embryonic soviets. Many of the leading militants involved in the engineering movement went on to join the Communist Party.

The terrible defeat of the 40-hour strike in 1919 and the engineers' lockout of 1922 killed off the shop stewards movement. As J T Murphy explained:

> *In England we have a powerful shop stewards movement. But it can and only does exist in given objective conditions. These conditions at the moment do not exist... You cannot build factory organisations in empty and depleted workshops, while you have a great reservoir of unemployed workers.*[40]

## The Communist Party and the rank and file in the 1930s

The defeat of the General Strike and mass unemployment ripped the heart out of the working class from 1926 onwards. By the mid-1930s the gradual fall in unemployment meant that the working class movement was slowly beginning to recover its confidence. The historian Richard Croucher writes, 'The effect of seeing old mates, even in ones and twos, coming back into the shops was out of all proportions to the numbers involved'.[41] The Communist Party had 6,263 members in 1931[42]—around 75 percent of those employed were manual workers.[43] In 1932 the Communist Party began to launch a number of rank and file groups. I want to take a look at two of them.

The most effective of these rank and file movements was found on the London buses. London bus workers, numbering nearly 25,000, belonged to the Transport and General Workers Union. Their full time officer was Ernest Bevin, a red baiter. When it was leaked that management were going to impose a wage cut and redundancies, it also came out that the union was going to recommend acceptance of management's proposals. The Communist Party launched a rank and file paper entitled *Busmen's Punch*. They had no more than 12 members on the bus fleet.[44] Chelverton Road garage called an unofficial meeting. Thirty-three garages were represented and they voted to set up a delegate committee, later to be known as the Rank and File Committee. It was made up of Communists, Labour Party members and militant trade unionists. The rank and file movement adopted a set of demands, which included a seven-hour day, no spreadovers and no standing passengers. *Busmen's Punch* described these demands as a 'fighting programme'.[45]

Bevin put the management's terms to ballot. The unofficial rank and file body campaigned hard against the wage cut. Members voted four to one to reject the offer. Bevin was forced to call an official strike. At this the company withdrew its threatened wage reductions and dismissals. It was a total victory for the rank and file. Over the next four years the Rank and File Committee led a number of small skirmishes with the bosses and the union. Sales of *Busmen's Punch* reached 10,000.[46] Rank and file activists issued an appeal to those not involved in the unofficial movement. It read:

> *Militancy is the stepping stone to progress. Organised militancy makes progress certain. The rank and file movement is organised militancy... The rank and file...stands for a 100 percent trade union, yet you know that permanent officials need gingering up. The rank and file movement puts the 'G' into ginger.*[47]

Within three years membership of the Communist Party on the London fleet reached 100. Importantly, the rank and file movement did not restrict itself to just sectional issues. It encouraged busmen to get involved in wider political issues. Large contingents of busmen were involved in the marches against Mosley and the British Union of Fascists, and the unofficial body also organised an energetic campaign to send aid to Republican Spain.

The battle for a shorter working week in 1937 led the unofficial movement into a major confrontation with the employers and the union. Bus workers put in a claim for a seven and a half hour day. Once again Bevin opposed the strike and once again the rank and file pushed for one. An all-out bus strike began on 1 May 1937. If the tram and trolley bus workers had been called out victory was assured, but the union refused. For four weeks the strikers held solid, but finally the union suspended the machinery of the bus section and called on the strikers to return to work.

The second example I want to look at is the aircraft industry. From 1934 increased aircraft orders generated by rearmament programmes gave renewed confidence to trade unionists in the industry to fight for improvements in pay and conditions. Union activists in the aircraft industry set up an Aircraft Shop Stewards National Council, which launched a monthly paper, *New Propellor*. Peter Zinkin, a full time industrial organiser for the Communist Party, edited it. The paper was sold throughout the aircraft industry and by 1937 its circulation reached 14,000.[48]

One of the first tasks the ASSNC undertook was to organise support for a series of unofficial strikes in Blackburn, Stockport and Hayes. In 1937 a group of young apprentices working on the Clyde walked out on strike against low pay and for the right to union representation. Within a week they had picketed out 13,000 young engineers. A committee of 160 representing every shop on strike was elected. The Young Communist League played a key role in the strike. The *New Propellor* produced a special youth edition. After four weeks management caved in. Apprentices in other regions followed the Clyde's example and also struck. The employers were forced to recognise the right of unions to negotiate on behalf of apprentices.

The networks of stewards organisations created on the buses, engineering and a large number of other industries became the backbone of the shop floor union organisation that lasted well into the 1960s and early 1970s. The Communist Party was a mass of contradictions. On the one hand, it recruited some of the most class-conscious workers and led a series of impressive strikes. On the other, it remained loyal to the Soviet regime and followed every twist and turn of Stalin's foreign policy. By the late 1930s the Communist Party dropped its rank and file strategy and adopted a policy of trying to get left wing officials elected into union positions. Sadly the Communist Party's change in line meant that instead of trying to 'ginger up' the full time officials, many of the best activists became the union officials that needed 'gingering up'.

**The 1970s: the rank and file movement last time**

The CP's timidity left many leading militants without a home. The increase of working class militancy meant a big vacuum opened up in the 1970s, which allowed the International Socialists (IS), the predecessor of the Socialist Workers Party, to grow rapidly. It was able to recruit a number of leading shop stewards. By 1974 the IS had 4,000 members and 40 factory branches. With the support of other trade union militants IS was able to launch a series of rank and file papers.

All in all there were 16 rank and file papers produced. They really tapped into the anger at the workplace. Nine issues of the *Car Worker* were produced, with sales of one edition peaking at 3,000. There were 12 issues of the *Dock Worker*, which at its height sold 5,000 copies, while *Rank and File Teacher* sold 4,000 copies. Alex Callinicos explains what followed:

> *In March 1974 the IS took its first step in initiating a national rank and file movement that would link together militants in different industries and operate, unlike the CP and the Broad Lefts, independently of the officials. A National Rank and File Organising Committee was set up and three delegate conferences were held—two in 1974 and one in 1977. The last was attended by 522 delegates from 251 trade union bodies, a perfectly respectable level of support.*[49]

But this national rank and file movement was stillborn. Its failure was partially due to the small industrial base the IS had compared to the Communist Party. But the main reason was that the confidence of the rank and file was subsiding—first under Labour and the Social Contract and secondly under the vicious anti-union onslaught undertaken by Thatcher.

**The emerging rank and file movement today**

In the post, health and rail the embryos of a new rank and file movement are beginning to develop. *Post Worker* now sells just over 5,000 copies. *Across the Tracks*, the rank and file paper for tube and rail workers, sold over 2,000, *The Car Worker* sold nearly 3,000 during the Vauxhall crisis and sales of *Health Worker* have now reached 2,000. The Socialist Workers Party has played a key role in helping launch these papers. This rank and file movement has begun to develop because of the political generalisation and the slow recovery of confidence that is taking place inside the working class. One other factor is also helping their development—the decline of the traditional Broad Lefts in many industries has provided a space for a new left to emerge.

It is worth looking at the rank and file *Post Worker* organisation in more detail. The editorial board of the *Post Worker* is made up of two CWU representatives elected from every region of the country. Activists have consciously attempted to make sure that the editorial board contains members with a wide range of political views—Labour Party, SWP, Scottish Socialist Party, Socialist Alliance, Welsh Socialist Alliance and workers who have no political allegiance. It has played an important role in agitating against privatisation and job cuts and has held a series of successful meetings in London, Edinburgh, Sheffield and Bristol.

The influence *Post Worker* has amongst activists was graphically shown during the unofficial strike last year. At its height 50,000 workers were involved. *Post Worker* produced a daily strike bulletin. One CWU rep wrote a letter to *Post Worker*. This is an extract from it:

> *Thank god for the* **Post Worker** *strike bulletin. Union HQ kept us totally in the dark. It was the only thing that kept us informed about what was going on. Not only did it counter management's lies, it kept our full time union officer in check. He was always eager to tell us that the strike was on the verge of collapsing.*[50]

*Post Worker* also rushed out two editions of its paper. Both had front pages written by the Merseyside Amal strike committee.[51]

## Conclusion

We live in exciting times. The anti-capitalist movement is back on track—the huge 80,000-strong event in Porto Alegre, Brazil, and the 20,000-strong march in New York showed that. New Labour's love affair with the neoliberal free market ideology shows no sign of abating. The Labour Party's own base continues to haemorrhage—last year membership fell by 30,000. A socialist electoral alternative to New Labour is beginning to take shape. The one missing element has been an increase in the level of industrial struggle. Now that recovery is clearly on the agenda.

Nothing is guaranteed. But one thing is certain—this is not going to be a repeat of the 1970s. The strong shop stewards movement that was the bane of the Heath government has been weakened. The Communist Party's hold on the shop stewards movement has all but vanished. But as these new struggles develop it is possible to forge a new shop stewards movement. This is not wishful thinking. We have seen it happen recently in the post office, on the rail and amongst electricians in the construction industry.

Other factors put socialists in a stronger position than perhaps they were in the 1970s. Labour's stranglehold over the movement is loosening. Not one single union discussed breaking its link with the Labour Party 30 years ago. Today four unions have started debating the possibility of breaking that link. This is not an act of despair. In all four unions the movers of the motions talked about using the money to fund genuine socialist parties. Also, imagine if activists could fuse the excitement and flair of the anti-capitalist movement with the potential power and organisation of the working class. That is not so far fetched—we saw it happen on the streets of Genoa in Italy last year. We also saw a glimpse of this on the Stop the War demonstrations in London last year.

Socialists have always been at the heart of any revival of working class militancy. Revolutionary socialists like Willie Gallagher and J T Murphy played a pivotal role in the first shop stewards movements on the Clyde and in Sheffield, while the Communist Party played a central role in rebuilding the shops stewards movement and fanning the flames of workplace militancy in the 1930s. Despite its relatively small size, the IS helped launch a vibrant rank and file movement. Today socialists have got to throw themselves into the developing struggles.

One of the great slogans of the anti-capitalist movement—even if it started out as a spoof—is, 'Get rid of capitalism and replace it with something nicer.' The problem is that even the most dynamic trade union organisation cannot do away with capitalism. At best, trade unions can limit the rate of exploitation workers suffer, and even the best rank and file movements cannot escape the booms and slumps of the capitalist economy. For that you need a revolutionary party—one that doesn't just fight over trade union questions but attempts to generalise the struggles, link them up and smash the capitalist state. To do that requires a party that is rooted in the working class, one that has activists in every branch of industry—agitating, organising and politically generalising from every struggle.

For more years than I care to remember, socialists in Britain have been enviously looking over the Channel at the industrial struggles in Europe. Now at last we are witnesses to the re-emergence of the working class in Britain. The union movement faces many hard battles and many defeats lie ahead. But for all that, the working class is beginning to move forward again.

**Notes**

1 I was present at a strikers' meeting on 4 February 2002 when a debate took place about the anti-capitalist movement in the strike.
2 I edit *Post Worker*.
3 TUC, *Migrant Workers: A TUC Guide*, January 2002.
4 TSSA conference report, Summer 2000.
5 G Hinsliff, 'Blair's Showdown With Unions On Privatisation', *The Observer*, 3 February 2002, p11.
6 J Pilger, *Daily Mirror*, 5 November 2001.
7 Labour Market Trends, *Trade Union Membership 1999-2000*, September 2001, p433.
8 Statistics gathered from the Employment Relations Directorate website, Department of Trade and Industry.

9 Statistic from a paper given by Tony Burke at a TUC conference on union recruitment, September 1999.
10 H A Clegg, *A History of British Trade Unions Since 1889*, vol 2 (Oxford, 1985), p570.
11 TUC, *Focus on Recognition*, trade union trends survey, January 2002.
12 C Adams and R Bennett, 'New Labour's Trial By Strike', *Financial Times*, 30 January 2002, p19.
13 Compiled from articles in *Socialist Worker*, 12 and 19 July 1997.
14 Compiled from articles in *Socialist Worker,* 1, 8 and 16 November 1997.
15 Compiled from articles in *The Car Worker*, April 2000 and January 2001.
16 Compiled from articles in *Health Worker*, May and June 2001.
17 Compiled from articles in *Across the Tracks,* rank and file paper for rail and tube workers, May 2001.
18 Compiled from articles in *Post Worker*, issues 4 and 5, May 2001.
19 L McKinstry, 'March Of The Hard Left', *Daily Mail*, 21 January 2002, p30.
20 R Bennett and C Adams, 'Ministers Try To Step Back From Post Row', *Financial Times*, 2 February 2002, p4.
21 C Adams and R Bennett, op cit, p19.
22 *Socialist Worker*, 19 January 2002, pp1, 4, 5.
23 K Marx, *The 18th Brumaire of Louis Bonaparte* (London, 1984), p10
24 For an interesting account of the rise of the white collar civil service unions you should read E Wigham, *From Humble Petition to Militant Action: A History of the Civil and Public Services Association 1903-1978* (London, 1980).
25 R Harrison, *Independent Collier* (Hassocks, 1978), p1.
26 T Cliff and D Gluckstein, *The Labour Party: A Marxist History* (London, 1988), p311.
27 J Rees, 'Anti-Capitalism, Reformism and Socialism', *International Socialism* 90 (Spring 2001), p23.
28 F Engels, *The Condition of the Working Class in England, 1844,* in K Marx and F Engels, *Collected Works,* vol 4 (London, 1984), p507.
29 T Cliff and D Gluckstein, op cit, p27.
30 T Baldwin and C Buckley, 'Power And The Purse', *The Times*, 27 June 2001, p10.
31 Statistics supplied by CWU.
32 Statistics supplied by PCS.
33 L Trotsky, *Writings on Britain,* vol 2 (London, 1974), p141.
34 Clyde Workers Committee leaflet in the Beveridge Collection, British Library of Political and Economic Science, section 3, item 5.
35 L Trotsky, op cit.
36 Figures supplied by Left Unity.
37 Figures supplied by United Left.
38 R Darlington, *Capital and Class* 76 (Spring 2002), p115.
39 The best account of the Great Unrest can be found in G Dangerfield, *The Strange Death of Liberal England* (London, 1997).
40 J T Murphy, *Preparing for Power* (London, 1972), pp129-130.
41 R Croucher, *Engineers at War* (London, 1982), p25.
42 N Fishman, *The British Communist Party and the Trade Unions, 1933-45*, (London, 1996), p345.
43 N Branson, *History of the Communist Party of Great Britain 1927-1941* (London, 1985), p83.
44 Ibid, p93.
45 N Fishman, op cit, p108.
46 N Branson, op cit, p175.
47 N Fishman, op cit, p117.
48 N Branson, op cit, p179.

49 A Callinicos, *Socialists in the Trade Unions* (London, 1995), p51.
50 Letter sent by a postal worker in Essex to the editorial board of *Post Worker*. It wasn't published but was posted on the website.
51 Compiled from articles in *Post Worker*, issues 4 and 5, May 2001.

# Crisis in Zimbabwe

LEO ZEILIG

Zimbabwe is in the middle of a major economic and political crisis. Supporters of the opposition, the Movement for Democratic Change, are routinely killed. Whole communities are intimidated while the government arms a militia—the Youth Brigades—which threatens even greater violence. Elliot Manyika, the country's youth minister, is setting up camps to indoctrinate youth so that they 'fully appreciate their country and stand by it in times of crisis'.[1] The government has pushed through legislation mimicking George Bush's 'war on terrorism' that makes it almost impossible to oppose the government. The Public Order and Security Act carries the death penalty for acts of 'insurgency, banditry, sabotage and terrorism'.[2] The army chief, General Vitalis Zvinavashe, has said that the army will refuse to recognise a government led by a person who is not a veteran of the war for independence, ruling out the opposition. At the same time the 'international community' led by Britain is virtually hysterical. New Labour politicians talk about Mugabe as a madman 'on the loose', a crisis 'driven by one man's ruthless campaign', and Zimbabwe as a symbol of the need to reorder Africa.[3] They talk about the importance of guaranteeing black and white harmony in a democratic Zimbabwe. Foreign secretary Jack Straw insists that it is 'our' responsibility not to 'let a great continent go down'.[4] There is not much to choose between the violence and repression of a dying regime, and the hypocrisy and colonial morality of New Labour.

For some time newspapers have written about 'anarchy' in Zimbabwe, headlines have proclaimed the 'Secret Plan To Evict All Whites' and 'Lawless Zimbabwe "Sliding Into Anarchy"'.[5] At the same time Mugabe, who was once happy to implement the policies of the IMF and World Bank, has been transformed into the despised tyrant of the continent, a 'monster' determined to unleash 'mob savagery' against law abiding (white) Zimbabweans.[6] But practically all of the recent coverage sees the crisis from the point of view of the devastation to white farmers in Zimbabwe, hysterical war veterans or 'mobs' rampaging mindlessly through the capital, Harare. Even on the left some have seen some truth in Mugabe as the new leader of the fight against imperialism and globalisation. Protesters outside the anti-racism conference in Durban, South Africa wore T-shirts emblazoned with the words 'Mugabe is right! Seize the land'.[7]

The picture in Zimbabwe is very different. Less than 5 percent of the population, a mix of black and white families and businesses, monopolise almost 70 percent of the nation's income. With 76 percent of the population on or below the poverty line, Zimbabwe is one of the world's most unequal societies.[8] The country is also facing its worst economic crisis since independence, with unemployment at over 60 percent and inflation hitting 114 percent. Employment in the formal sector has collapsed, leaving thousands of graduates without work or the prospect of getting any. Female students are pushed into prostitution to pay for their studies and food in privatised dinner halls at the University of Zimbabwe. Fuel and food prices are forcing rural communities to move into overcrowded shanty towns on the outskirts of the two major cities, Harare and Bulawayo, while families already living in urban areas face a constant struggle to feed themselves. A quarter of the adult population is infected with AIDS, making Zimbabwe one of the worst affected countries in the world, but healthcare, largely decimated by IMF and World Bank policies, cannot cope with or treat patients dying from the disease.[9]

The country is also embroiled in the war in the Democratic Republic of Congo (DRC), involving more than 15,000 troops, a quarter of the entire army. Army generals and businessmen have been rewarded with contracts on mines and in logging companies. Mugabe's support for the government of the DRC has been rewarded by the gift of vast areas of the land. One company, run by leading members of the ruling party Zimbabwe African National Union—Patriotic Front (ZANU-PF), has been granted what Global Witness calls 'the world's largest logging concession by gaining rights to exploit 33 million hectares of forests'—an area ten times the size of Switzerland.[10]

However, since 1995 Zimbabwe has been rocked by mass struggles which have threatened the regime and the interests of Western imperialism and neo-liberalism. These struggles have received virtually no attention in most mainstream accounts of the crisis, which prefer to see the current situation arising out of Mugabe's autocratic rule. As one activist observes, 'The main point I want to make is that we were on the verge of a sort of revolution in Zimbabwe'.[11]

Out of these upheavals came one of the most powerful opposition movements on the continent. The Movement for Democratic Change (MDC) emerged out of the Zimbabwe Congress of Trade Unions (ZCTU) in 1999 and became the most important force to challenge Mugabe since independence in 1980. The party almost won the parliamentary election in 2000, winning 57 seats, despite widespread violence by the ruling ZANU-PF which cost 31 lives. The fact that it came close to toppling such a violent regime after having only existed for 16 months is an indication of the extent of the changes sweeping Zimbabwean society.[12]

But the MDC is an enigma. While it was formed by the leadership of the ZCTU—Morgan Tsvangirai and Gibson Sibanda—it includes industrialists and white farmers, and a constellation of smaller pressure groups and left wing parties. Eddie Cross, the party's spokesperson on economic matters, is a well known entrepreneur who champions privatisation and the policies of the IMF and World Bank. It has also received funding from the Tories, and when presented with the party's economic programme the World Bank reportedly said, 'We would have been proud to produce a programme like this, let alone have it handed to us'.[13] How long this alliance of forces will hold together is a central question in Zimbabwe today.

What has happened in Zimbabwe in recent years that has led to these events? What are the roots of the crisis? Why is the question of land so important? And, crucially for us, what role have Zimbabwean workers played in the struggles that have rocked the country?

## The rise and fall of Rhodesia

Zimbabwe has one of the most important economies in Africa. Unlike most African countries it has fairly well developed industrial and agricultural sectors. It has a relatively developed infrastructure, and it produces a range of goods in a number of industries. Manufacturing, at 24.8 percent of GDP in 1990, was about three times higher than most African countries. The sector employed 16.5 percent of all those in the formal economy. Agriculture is also diversified, growing such crops as tobacco, wheat, beef and cotton. Coupled with this is a massive concentration of ownership and control that originates from the state set up by the British more than 100 years ago. Almost 60 percent of industrial production is controlled by foreign capital while, until recently, only 4,000 mostly white farmers controlled 70 percent of the most fertile land, forcing more than 7 million peasants onto dry and drought-ridden plots.[14]

What are the origins of this situation? Zimbabwe emerged out of the authoritarian and racist state established by the British over a century ago. In 1890 the territory was marked out and handed to the imperialist adventurer Cecil Rhodes. He controlled the area for his British South Africa Company. The British confronted wave after wave of resistance culminating in the eventual defeat of *Chimurenga*—the anti-colonial revolt in 1898. The following 40 years witnessed the mass expropriation of land from peasant farmers and communities, the repression of any form of resistance, and forced labour on mines and in factories. Thousands of Africans were forced off their land and herded into what were called communal lands, or reservations. The racial land division was consolidated by two pieces of legislation, the Land Apportionment Act of 1930 and the Land Tenure Act of 1969, both of which prohibited Africans from owning land in white areas.[15] When Mugabe came to power 97 percent of the population was confined to a quarter of the land.[16]

In 1927 the Industrial and Commercial Workers Union (ICU) was established as the country's first trade union. It was founded principally by migrant workers from South Africa. Large numbers of white workers were recruited in both Britain and South Africa to work on the railways and mines. These groups of workers were initially responsible for a high level of militancy, leading strikes, and even forming a Rhodesian Labour Party, inspired by the British labour movement.[17]

In 1923 Rhodes's company rule was ended and limited self government was granted to Southern Rhodesia. The Reform Party, a coalition of British interests, dominated the political scene, and sought to solidify an alliance between an increasingly militant white working class and the state. Only white workers were allowed to strike or belong to unions, although they were not allowed to form independent trade unions.

By the late 1920s the dye was set for the next 50 years. White workers became wedded to the Rhodesian state, splitting the working class on racial and craft lines. Even so, a small Southern Rhodesian Communist Party emerged from a left wing faction of the Labour Party. However, it was soon paralysed by following Russia's advice to form 'popular fronts'. Agitation amongst African workers was deemed provocative to building these cross-class alliances.[18]

The state managed to force through a high level of industrialisation from the 1930s onwards. In the 1950s, for example, annual growth was 10 percent. But as the economy expanded, so did the African working class. By 1950 the industrial working class, concentrated in urban areas around the industrial centre of what are today Bulawayo and Harare, had reached

469,000.[19] The 1948 general strike was the first major confrontation that threatened the state and gave life to the nationalist movement.

At the beginning of April 1948 a derisory wage offer was made by the Rhodesian Federal Chamber of Commerce. On 8 April at a mass meeting in Bulawayo police spies reported a 'mass in favour of going on strike'. The Southern Rhodesian African National Congress (SRANC), which had been set up in the 1930s, persuaded workers to postpone action until a meeting in July. When the SRANC made the same suggestion a few days later the meeting 'refused to listen to the leaders and finally broke up in disorder [with] everyone shouting, "Strike! Strike!"'.[20]

The next day pickets prevented workers leaving locations while others travelled to urban areas to spread the action. On 14 April the mass of workers in Bulawayo had joined the strike. Before long the strike movement had spread to the capital, Salisbury. One strike leader complained that 'extremists' were determined to subvert the strike: 'I will use the word "extremists" meaning groups of Africans who probably organised the strike in secret and were opposed to any actions I took, and did their very best to influence strikes against me'.[21] Another witness to the strike described it as 'the first strike which threatened the white man'.[22]

Despite its militancy the strike illustrated a weakness in the working class. Although there were African organisations in Southern Rhodesia by the late 1940s, there was not, in the words of one commentator, a 'single organisation which was able to co-ordinate and unify the struggles of Africans'.[23] This meant that elitist, even conservative forces could come to the fore. Benjamin Burumbo, a local shop owner who became a leader of the strike, falsely assured a meeting of strikers that the government had increased their wages in line with their demands. He became a leading figure in the nationalist movement. Mkushi Khumalo, an activist during 1948, described Burumbo in the following terms:

> *Burumbo was not an employee. Those who associate him with the strike are making a mistake. He was simply an opportunist... Burumbo decided to join us and went about giving speeches as if he were an employee, and yet in fact he was a businessman, an employer. It was under these circumstances that Burumbo became a participant in the strike.*[24]

The period demonstrated the failure, partly as a result of the political paralysis caused by Stalinism, to build an independent socialist organisation that could develop and lead the African working class. At each point of this failure, during the general strike in 1948 and later throughout the 1960-1961 *Zhii* strike movement, other political forces and classes were able to capitalise on the organisational vacuum left by the working class. Benjamin Burumbo managed to force himself on the movement, helping ultimately to return the country to the authorities. Joshua Nkomo, the railway union leader, was also a representative of the same phenomenon. He was a young graduate who had made his name in the 1948 general strike, sponsored by the railways in the hope that he could help offset the growth of radicalism. He rose to become the leading figure in nationalist politics in the 1950s and 1960s. The dearth of socialist politics allowed a group of educated Africans, a petty bourgeoisie, to lead a movement that had the potential of far greater liberation.[25]

The 1948 strikes did, however, provide the impetus for the formation of the first trade union congress, and in 1954 the Southern Rhodesia Trade Union Congress (SRTUC) was founded. It was headed by Joshua Nkomo. This in turn precipitated the creation three years later of an overtly nationalist organisation, the African National Congress (ANC). Trade unionists were the main source of support, and trade union leaders occupied most of the main positions in the organisation. Nkomo became the organisation's first president. After the ANC was banned in 1959, Nkomo formed the Zimbabwe African Peoples Union (ZAPU).

In 1962 the Rhodesian Front, a right wing party headed by the racist Ian Smith, won power. Smith declared independence from Britain in 1965, in what was called a Unilateral Declaration of Independence (UDI). The decision was made in the context of the growth of resistance in Rhodesia and the rising politicisation across the continent which came with independence movements. The white minority sought to ensure their supremacy by supporting Smith in a continent that seemed to be turning the white man out. Nkomo sought active intervention against this decision from the UK government, and although British courts condemned UDI as 'treasonable' the Labour prime minister Harold Wilson refused to intervene.

Radical members of the nationalist movement, including Mugabe, broke with Nkomo to form the Zimbabwe African National Union (ZANU). By the 1970s the fight against white minority rule was led by a left wing intelligentsia informed by Maoist and Stalinist ideas. They focused on guerrilla war in the countryside. This was reasonably successful, and by the end of 1970s the Patriotic Front forces were somewhere between 35,000 and 40,000 strong. The government's forces were engaged on approximately six fronts, with martial law imposed throughout the whole country.[26] Although these tactics achieved some success, they failed to win a decisive victory over Smith and the Rhodesian Front. For those fighting against the Rhodesians there was an additional risk—even in the middle of the war Mugabe was murdering his opponents in the liberation struggle.[27] Ian Smith was finally forced to negotiate and, largely under pressure from Mozambique, Mugabe accepted the Lancaster House agreement. In 1980 Zimbabwe became independent.

## Land, independence and reconciliation

Zimbabwean independence involved one of the most spectacular and instant reconciliations in the history of armed conflict. The 1979 Lancaster House agreement that led directly to independence the following year guaranteed the property of the small white population. Ian Smith's regime conceded to black majority rule on the basis of a promise that the property rights of the white majority would be safeguarded, and that when land reform eventually came white farmers would be fully compensated. At the same time Robert Mugabe and Joshua Nkomo, the two leaders of the independence war, were persuaded to adopt a new constitution that prevented the forced expropriation of white farms for ten years. This was a far cry from Mugabe's promise a few years before that 'none of the white exploiters will be allowed to keep an acre of their land'. This promise was extracted with the 'commitment' from the Thatcher government to make hundreds of millions available for land reform in the future.[28]

However, the only official commitment secured by the foreign secretary, Lord Carrington, was that the first government would not be able to confiscate white property. Nevertheless Mugabe went on to win the election with the pledge that thousands of black families would be settled on white land within three years. The initial resettlement figure was for 162,000 families. In the end only 70,000 families were resettled in that period. However, the 1980s did see a certain amount of successful resettlement, which was often popularly driven through a large number of 'illegal' occupations. The period that followed was notable for its failure to continue the limited progress that had been made.[29]

Despite the lapse of the constitutional block on compulsory purchase in 1990, the regime failed to pursue redistribution with any seriousness. There are three principal reasons. Firstly, the huge profits made from export crops by white farmers were a major disincentive to pursue large-scale resettlement. Secondly, the priority during this period was to expand black commercial farmland, a process of 'indigenisation', but this was coupled with confusion about whether the problems of communal areas could be resolved through expanded resettlement. Finally, and crucially, the adoption of a structural adjustment programme in the early 1990s led to a massive reduction of public expenditure on social programmes which were essential to the resettlement projects.

Another important factor was the relationship of the regime to white farmers. White farmers, and the white community generally, never integrated socially or politically with the black population after independence.

However, they were not the present day 'colonialists' and 'imperialists' (as they are labelled by Mugabe), but rather useful allies to the regime.[30] As a consequence, 20 years after independence the percentage of white land resettled by black families was a fraction of the total land owned by the white population, while most of the money promised at the 'gentlemen's agreement' in London years before failed to appear. From the hundreds of millions promised by the British only a meagre £44 million ever materialised and, like all aid, it came with conditions, meaning that after the wrangling about what it could be used on, not even all of this sum was spent.

Some of the land that was redistributed in the early 1990s was used to create a class of black commercial farmers. Although there were certainly a number of questionable deals over the allocation of land to black commercial farmers, at this point not all of the land went to political friends. Yet the combined effect of structural adjustment and the wave of popular protests after 1996 decisively shifted the pattern and use of land allocation. Two hundred farms were purchased and distributed to army officers and party officials whose loyalty could be guaranteed with the promise of land. One giant estate was parcelled into 27 smaller farms and presented to a handful of party figures, including presidential spokesman George Charamba. The military also benefited—General Vitalis Zvinavashe received his own estate while thousands of poor Zimbabweans were ignored. In the recent land grab it is again political patronage that has determined allocation. Loyal reporters, leading politicians and soldiers have been given land, but title deeds have remained with the government, ensuring continued loyalty to the regime. Still the pattern of current commercial land allocation is a small part of the total picture and it is important to remember that recent land occupations have often been popularly driven, and the government has sought desperately to control them.[31]

The compromises, procrastination and ultimately the failure to confront the issue of land redistribution are representative of the general approach of the regime. In the immediate aftermath of independence Mugabe made his intentions clear. He asserted that there would be no fundamental transformation of society and, despite the change in government, white businesses and farmers could rest assured that their living conditions would be guaranteed. On 17 April 1980, in front of an international crowd that included Prince Charles, Robert Gabriel Mugabe reassured the country:

> *If yesterday I fought you as an enemy, today you have become a friend. If yesterday you hated me, today you cannot avoid the love that binds you to me and me to you.*[32]

For a time the desire to seek reconciliation and restore confidence to white farmers and businesses looked as though it would bring down the government.[33] As one writer observed, 'Despite its Marxist-Leninist rhetoric the ZANU-PF government tried to preserve the largely white-owned productive structures'.[34] The gross inequalities of ownership and control in the economy were maintained and shored up after independence.

It was not simply the inequalities that remained after independence, but much of the Rhodesian state. A great deal of the colonial legal system remained intact, ensuring unparallelled powers for the president and the ruling party. The state continued to suppress dissent—it labelled oppositionists terrorists and massacred 'enemy' communities. The recent violence expresses the continuity and escalation of state repression, not its first appearance. The worst examples of this brutality were the massacres in Matabeleland in the 1980s. The majority of the population were Ndebele speakers who were regarded as supporters of the rival liberation organisation ZAPU, led by Nkomo. It has been estimated that between 1981 and 1988 between 10,000 and 20,000 'dissidents'—the normal euphemism for unarmed civilians—were killed. Thousands more were herded into concentration camps, raped, tortured and starved.[35]

At independence the union movement was fragmented and disorganised. Yet in the first years of independence there was an upsurge of strike action—200 strikes were officially recorded between 1980 and 1981.[36] In many ways these strikes contained the grievances of a generation. Although many were concerned with low wages, other strikes were against racist managers and the discrimination against trade union representation. The strikes helped to ensure that the government implemented a number of important reforms in the next few years.

Later on the government urged the merger of unions into a central federation, the Zimbabwe Congress of Trade Unions (ZCTU). To start with, the ZCTU was tied closely to the government. The ZCTU was packed with Mugabe's friends, and even a member of his family. This relationship persisted while the government implemented limited reforms—a national minimum wage, legislation enshrining labour rights, and health and education provision.

For a few years in the early 1980s the government increased spending on health and education, and picked up considerable support both in towns and the countryside. Between 1980 and 1990 primary and secondary schools were built across Zimbabwe. Enrolment increased in primary education from 1.2 million in 1980 to more than 2.2 million by 1989, and in secondary schools from only 74,000 to 671,000 in the same period.[37] However, by the mid-1980s the economy had begun to stagnate. From 1986-1987 per capita GDP declined rapidly.[38] Loans from the World Bank, happily and greedily accepted by the government, caused foreign debt to rise from $786 million in 1980 to $3 billion in 1990.[39] Having precipitated the crisis a group of neo-liberals gathered around the finance and economics minister, Bernard Chidzero. Thus under some duress, but not without complicity, the government invited the World Bank in to reorganise the economy. Supporters of the state capitalist reforms of the early years became marginalised.[40]

## Structural adjustment

The government introduced the first full Economic Structural Adjustment Programme (ESAP) in 1991, although the IMF had been pressing the government to reduce expenditure and devalue the Zimbabwe dollar from as early as 1982.[41] Following similar—and similarly disastrous—programmes in most of Africa the World Bank insisted on trade liberalisation, the removal of import controls and export incentives, deregulation—including changes to what was regarded as 'restrictive' labour legislation—and widespread public sector reforms. The effects were devastating.[42]

The government now pursued policies involving privatisation and the closure of state companies deemed unprofitable by Western donors, the IMF and the World Bank. The year after the implementation of the ESAP saw a huge 11 percent fall in per capita GDP.[43] More than 20,000 jobs were lost between January 1991 and July 1993. In 1993 unemployment had reached a record 1.3 million from a total population of about 10 million.[44] Tor Skalnes reported 25,000 civil service jobs lost by 1995, while 'inflation rose and exports declined'.[45] The new policies promoted by Washington and the IMF failed to stem, and by all accounts helped to deepen, the recession that continued to grip Zimbabwe.

A new militancy was born out of this turmoil. By the late 1980s sections of society that had previously been termed 'middle class' were radicalised by the fall in living standards. At the same time opposition at the University of Zimbabwe emerged, criticising the rightward shift in government policy. Most significant was the rupture between the government and the trade union leadership. The old leadership of the ZCTU that had followed and supported the government since independence was replaced by a new one that was influenced by the radicalisation in society. In 1988 Tsvangirai—a mineworker and activist—became general secretary of the ZCTU. The following year he supported student protests at the University of Zimbabwe and was detained for six weeks on the suspicion of being a South African spy. The period was crucial for a new generation of militants and trade unionists. As Tendai Biti argues, 'It was the first time people criticised the legitimacy of these heroes. It showed you can make noise and not get killed'.[46]

While Mugabe's stories about the role he played in the struggle for national liberation had carried some weight in the 1980s, they now seemed more like the tales of an old man anxious to divert attention from the failure of that liberation. Most Zimbabweans only had access to infertile and barren land, and more often were landless labourers for white farmers who were protected by the government from the land invasions by angry workers and peasants. And those who had only been children during the struggle for independence were now the new working class, who had been brought up under a black government. They saw through Mugabe's hollow promises and began to mobilise for change. The trade union bureaucracy even proclaimed during the 1991 May Day rally, 'Are we going to make 1991 the year of the World Bank storm?'[47] Later the ZCTU produced an alternative economic plan, 'Beyond ESAP', opposing some of the government's IMF-sponsored programme. But in the liberal rhetoric of 'Beyond ESAP' lay warning signs for those hoping for radicalism from the new union leadership.

## The upheavals

It was not until the mid-1990s that Zimbabwe experienced its first significant upheavals against the austerity policies pursued by the government. Many activists regard the demonstration against police brutality in 1995, triggered by the murder of several people by the police in Harare, as a turning point. One activist, Luke Kasuwanga, who helped to organise the demonstration, recalls how it inspired him:

> *When I reached home I waited for the 8 o'clock news. The news was read—Harare was burning! You could see fire everywhere. The minister was interviewed and we could see that he was sweating. He was saying, 'We know the people responsible and we are going to get them. They are going to pay for it.' And it all came under my name... At first you have to deny that you are involved* [but] *later on we are proud that we were at the forefront. And funnily enough one of my workmates—who wasn't involved in politics—he attended that demonstration, and that demonstration made him solid from that period... Why am I saying this? It politicised me. That was the first time being in the leading role whilst I was a worker not even having so much confidence.*

But it was not until 1996 that Zimbabwean society experienced mass struggle. In August there was the first national government workers' strike. Tens of thousands came out on strike against job losses, bad working conditions and government corruption. Although health workers, nurses and doctors initiated the strike, it spread rapidly to other workers—teachers, civil servants and almost every branch of the public sector. It affected every area of the country and crippled the government.

As the strike continued it developed clearly political aims, eventually even demanding a reduction in the size of the cabinet.

An elected committee of rank and file trade unionists directed the strike. Flying pickets moved from workplace to workplace arguing with workers to join the movement. Tafadzwa Choto, who was active at the time, recognised the importance of the period: 'I think the turning point was the government workers' strike in 1996. It really gave confidence to so many workers.'

Trade union leaders ran to keep up with the strike. Before long they forced themselves to the front of the movement and eventually persuaded strikers to accept a government offer. The strike ended in an agreement that included a large increase in wages, the promise of a new labour act, a guarantee that workers would receive bonuses, and the recognition of public sector unions. However, the agreement did not hold. By November health sector workers were on strike again, staying out until February 1997.[48]

If Zimbabwe's rulers thought the worst was over they would be sorely disappointed. The following year saw more demonstrations and strikes than at any time since independence. Students combined with workers who linked the struggle in the city with the need to distribute land in the countryside. As Tendai Beti, a leading activist at the time, remembers, 'This was a momentous occasion in the history of this country because it brought confidence—you could smell working class power in the air'.[49] Rural labourers and peasants invaded commercial farms in various provinces and tried to resist the police who had been sent by the ruling ZANU-PF to evict them and restore 'law and order'. A radicalised urban working class helped fuel the rural struggle.

The previously marginalised war veterans broke onto the scene. They were for the most part former fighters from the guerrilla war against the Rhodesian state. They had been abandoned since independence, and by the mid-1990s most of them were unemployed, without pensions or land. Galvanised by the mass upheavals shaking society, they joined demonstrations and started making their own demands. They denounced Mugabe at public forums, including at the annual Heroes' Commemoration.[50]

By the end of the year Mugabe was so frightened by the threat posed by the war veterans that he imposed a tax, a War Veterans' Levy, which he argued would be used to fund pensions for those who had fought in the war. As a result another strike, a two-day stayaway, was called by the ZCTU. Thousands of demonstrators converged on Harare, and by the end of the strike the government had agreed to remove the proposed tax. The wave of militancy that had started in 1996 continued into 1998. The year started with a 'bread riot' led by housewives, provoked by an increase in the cost of basic commodities. It frightened the government.

As the minister of home affairs commented immediately after the riots, 'The just-ended three-day food riots which came soon after the announcement of the general increase of prices of basic commodities, mealie meal, rice, cooking oil and bread, represent the most violent riots the country has experienced since independence'.[51]

Eight people were killed, hundreds injured and thousands of people arrested. The riots quickly combined workers and the unemployed, while leaders in the ZCTU tried to dissuade workers from joining the demonstrations.[52]

The union congress was not completely wrong-footed. The general secretary, Morgan Tsvangirai, understood the importance of the new wave of militancy. He even called for a general strike without consulting the general council of the congress, and was almost removed as a result. Kasuwanga illustrates the way the movement took the lead:

> *When ZCTU was calling for stayaways, these stayaways were called after the housewives and the unemployed were rioting in the townships spreading around Zimbabwe. Even the 1998 bread demonstrations, which shook the whole of Zimbabwe* [were] *done by housewives on their own. Even Tsvangirai said he was nothing to do with it. It began spontaneously on its own.*

The war veteran leader Chenjerai Hunzvi became a key loyalist to Mugabe during the period, even though his 'profile' as a middle class and privileged member of the establishment could not contrast more with the peasants and ex-combatants he now led.[53]

The ZCTU was mindful of events that had led to the removal of Kenneth Kaunda in neighbouring Zambia in the early 1990s. A movement led and organised by the Zambian Congress of Trade Unions had swept the old regime from power in elections held in 1991. The Movement for Multi-Party Democracy (MMD) came to power headed by Frederick Chiluba, the general secretary of the only trade union federation that had helped to co-ordinate strikes and demonstrations that undermined the old regime.[54] Already the level of militancy in Zimbabwe had surpassed the mass struggles that had transformed Zambian politics. But would Zimbabwe follow the same path? What should the ZCTU do?

## A workers' party?

Between 1996 and 1998 the ZCTU repeatedly sought to lead and direct a mass movement that persistently pre-empted their direction. Rank and file activists, often organising in labour forums (where large groups of workers meet to discuss politics) rushed ahead of union bureaucrats in organising strikes and demonstrations. From 1998 a recurrent theme of the labour forums was the demand for the ZCTU to form a workers' party, a demand that was repeatedly rejected on the grounds that a union's work should be limited to 'economic' and not 'political' issues. However, as the crisis deepened so did the urgency of these demands.

Meanwhile Mugabe seemed to be failing everyone. The 'international community' who had long regarded him as a reliable partner, and Zimbabwe as proof of the efficacy of IMF and World Bank reforms, began to ostracise the regime. He caved in too easily to an audacious workers' movement, which was meant to have been subdued by ten years of World Bank led reforms. Gradually various NGOs, academics, businessmen and lawyers added their voices to the calls for a new opposition. The 'demands' now carried a contradiction. On the one hand they came from below, the labour forums and the streets that had been involved in mass struggle since 1996. These forces insisted on a reversal of Mugabe's 'privatisation and patience'. But on the other hand pressure was mounted by the middle class—academics, lawyers and businesses who were threatened by the movement they now sought to co-opt.

Mugabe began to realise that if he was going to survive where Kaunda and Malawi's Hastings Kamuza Banda—also ejected by popular resistance—had not, then he must be seen to retreat from an agenda of IMF reform that he had enthusiastically defended. The regime moved quickly, and government rhetoric began to lambast 'imperialism' and 'Western racism'. The effects of this shift helped to consolidate middle class and foreign support for a 'new party', in opposition to Mugabe's new position. ZANU-PF did not move forward in one mass. Factions in the party, principally around Eddison Zvobgo, a longstanding advocate of neo-liberal reform, became a focus of opposition in ZANU-PF, trying and ultimately failing to resist Mugabe.

Land was key to this reorientation. For nearly 20 years the government had failed to seriously redistribute land to the black majority starved of it. The government, which in the mid-1990s had ejected 'squatters' from occupied white farms, a few years later sanctioned the occupation by squatters of the same farms.[55] Mugabe began to realise the potential of the war veterans and used Hunzvi—'Hitler' as he labelled himself—to win their loyalty. Before long Mugabe had outmanoeuvred the opposition in his party and won most of the regime behind his new stance. The collapse in value of the Zimbabwean dollar at the end of 1998 was symbolic of what was to come—the isolation and rapid demonisation of the regime by international capital.

The call for a new party was finally answered. In March 1999 the Movement for Democratic Change (MDC), which was initially just a 'movement', was born through the National Working People's Convention (NWPC). The ZCTU had convened the NWPC, and invited NGOs, civic groups and residents' associations. However, the convention was not a friendly gathering, and attempts were made to exclude leading socialists. Tim Chitambure remembers:

> *The guys were given special instructions, 'You should not allow socialists in.' But you know what we did? We are the leading people in locations, so some went under the banner of residents' associations, some went under the banner of other groups in the National Constitutional Assembly (NCA).*

The aim for many of those present was to form a labour party committed to defending the interests of the working class, but the tension between these activists and the other participants was never far from the surface. As Chitambure remembers:

> *So we were saying that ZCTU should form a workers' party. But they didn't like it—they wanted to separate economics from politics... They asked: 'How come you are in here?' and you say, 'I am representing Glenfield residents association.' Those that did not get in were outside with some leaflets saying, 'In this convention push these points'.*[56]

Until the organisation's official launch in September 1999 the party was dominated by trade unionists, but a middle class bloc representing local and international business interests quickly began to encroach on the leadership of the party. In the parliamentary elections in June 2000 workers made up only 15 percent of the candidates. Policy also shifted, and the party courted Western leaders and committed itself in the election manifesto to policies of the 'free market', 'privatisation', 'direct investment' and land reform that succeeded in being to the right of ZANU-PF, offering only very limited redistribution to the poor.

The parliamentary vote followed the MDC victory in a referendum on a draft constitution proposed by the government in Feburary. The MDC almost won the parliamentary elections. For a party less than one and a half years old this was an extraordinary result. The party attracted the core of the urban working class in all of the principal cities—Harare, Bulawayo and Chitungwiza. But the election also marked a decisive shift in policy and symbolised the end of what had seemed to be the inextricable radicalisation of the struggle.[57]

How could the MDC have fallen into the hands of the middle class? The answer is the same weakness of the organised working class that we saw in the 1948 general strike. Although the ZCTU had jettisoned the old leadership in the late 1980s, its new leaders were still tied to Stalinist politics. When the regimes in Eastern Europe and Russia collapsed, so did the ideological signposts for a generation of trade union bureaucrats, activists and leaders. At the same time there was no clear organisational or ideological force in the working class with enough influence to make sense of these events. Although the period 1996-1998 showed the power, initiative and creative force of the Zimbabwean working class, the strikes and demonstrations remained ultimately under the control of the trade union bureaucracy. In turn they ensured that 'stayaways' would only be used as a means to, at most, pressurise Mugabe while keeping the interests of national and international capitalism on board.

But there was another element to the participation of the middle class in the MDC which was tied inextricably to the struggles that had marked the late 1990s. Kasuwanga argues that it was the threat of mass revolt and revolution that marginalised and frightened the middle class. These tensions forced them to respond to the MDC, as he explains:

> *The main point I want to make is that we were on the verge of a sort of revolution in Zimbabwe. There was going to be anarchy, whereby revolts were going to be happening any time, any day. So I think some interested groups, to stop this, said, 'Why don't you form this NCA and later on the MDC?' ... Through...the ZCTU calling for that dialogue thing* [it] *was trying to neutralise the power of workers. Because workers by then were calling* [for] *a five-day stayaway, the five-day stayaway was the one needed by workers. And Tsvangirai was calling for one day, two days, one day, two days, every Wednesday. It was a form of trying to control workers. If the MDC was not formed workers were going to revolt on their own. And the middle classes were scared. Do you know what was happening? People like me, I don't have O-levels, I don't have a degree. I was even more influential in my area. Our comrades, those who were putting up the barricades in the street, were having more influence. The 'middle class' were losing influence because no one could hear them. They couldn't stand and talk to the people rioting because the language was different. But having that dialogue thing, they try to interpret all of those things to us—the rule of law, the IMF, economics, 'We want foreign currency. We want this and that.' They thought that they were talking to the uneducated: 'You cannot understand this. Do this and do that.' That is how the struggle was stolen from our hands.*

Whether the strikes and mass struggles between 1996 and 1998 amounted to a 'revolutionary situation' is debatable. There were never consistent political demands under an independent leadership that could have made the question of state power and the forcible removal of Mugabe more than an issue among a minority of those active. But Kasuwanga is undoubtedly right that Zimbabwe went through a 'sort of revolution'.

Each step of the way attempts were made to stifle the independent voice of the movement. Organisations that had built solidarity, organised labour forums, set up tenants' associations, and participated in strikes and demonstrations were obstructed in their work. Despite this, the International Socialist Organisation (ISO) won an important seat in a working class area of Harare in the 2000 parliamentary elections as part of the MDC and, despite continued opposition from the party leadership, remains in the organisation.[58] However, regardless of the avowedly Blairite stance of the party, it is the product of the mass struggle that gripped Zimbabwe, and it is still regarded by the majority who participated in that struggle as the only means to get rid of Mugabe.[59]

## Conclusion

Zimbabwe today is an oddly familiar place—a government determined to rid the country of 'terrorists' who, they declare, are no more than agents of foreign powers, determined to subvert the integrity of a sovereign nation. There is more than a whiff of Rhodesia in the air. At the same time there is a chorus of, 'I told you Zimbabwe (and South Africa) would never last.' Countries that had shown so much promise before (in white hands) were destined to go the way of the continent. This of course is racist nonsense. It is, on the contrary, the continuity, not the rupture with colonial practices, that characterises the regime. Recent violence is built on what Mugabe claims to be fighting—the colonial legacy.

The British government were the authors of this legacy, and they have not changed. On the brink of war with Afghanistan, Tony Blair declared that the state of Africa was 'a scar on the conscience of the world'. He called for a new initiative for the continent that would involve a partnership with Africa. On the Western side it would involve more aid, less debt and 'training to soldiers'. On the African side it would involve good government, less tolerance of corruption and the activities 'of Mugabe's henchmen in Zimbabwe'. This is a sham, a wolf in sheep's clothing. The first 'initiative' the British state offered Africa was the colonisation of the continent more than 100 years ago. Since then British companies have profited in every conceivable way from what the great Guyanese scholar Walter Rodney termed 'how Europe underdeveloped Africa'.[60] The current agents of this underdevelopment, of which Tony Blair is an outspoken advocate, are the structural adjustment programmes and loans from the World Bank and the IMF. These helped to fund the genocidal regime in Rwanda and enrich corrupt governments like Mugabe's, while decimating healthcare that could have acted as a bulwark against the spread of AIDS. Solutions cannot be found in Western 'initiatives' or any form of recolonisation, but through the struggles of those who have resisted the policies of both Blair and Mugabe in Zimbabwe.

Mugabe's partial withdrawal from ESAP was not a principled decision based on socialist politics, but a cynical move forced on him by a political crisis caused by popular resistance and working class struggles. The reality for most Zimbabweans has been a continuation of the same policies, while the regime mouths platitudes about 'foreign powers' and 'racist imperialism'. Privatisation continues, the cost of fuel and food rises, while compensation packages for white farmers are hammered out by Commonwealth leaders who debate endlessly whether Zimbabwe should be excluded from their club. Unemployment now affects much more than half of the population—jobs in the 'formal' sector for new graduates and students have all but dried up. The increase in the price of food has meant that thousands of workers and the poor are forced to live on a diet of rice.

Although there is uncertainty about what will happen, it is clear that Mugabe will not tolerate defeat. Yet he is preparing for it. The government has created a paramilitary force among sections of the war veterans and the unemployed (attracting thousands with the offer of free food and lodging) to be called on to prevent defeat—or, in the event of it, to destabilise the country.[61] The choice for ordinary Zimbabweans has already been shown. It is the return to *Jambanja*, mass struggle, which offers the key. Morgan Tsvangirai threatened to remove Mugabe in 2000 by extra-parliamentary activity if he refused to go legally. As Choto says, 'Last year Tsvangirai made statements that Mugabe was going to be removed—if he didn't resign he was going to be removed by violence, and there was going to be mass action. That never took place, and the reason? The MDC was given advice by European countries not to do so.' His international backers were scared about the consequences of letting the *djinn* of mass protests out of the bottle. But it is this *djinn* that offers Zimbabwe the way out of the crisis.

There are many signs that a new radicalisation is already taking place. It is testimony to how quickly the situation is changing that a previously middle class organisation like the National Constitutional Assembly has moved massively to the left as the MDC swings further to the right. Activists in the NCA, anxious not to have only MDC loyalists on the steering committee, put forward an alternative slate in elections at a meeting in July 2001. Every member of this slate was elected, including two socialists. At the same time MPs for the MDC have been attacked by activists at meetings for 'selling out', and even Tsvangirai is booed and threatened by those who months ago used to cheer him. Disillusionment with the MDC is growing before the election, in a way similar to the situation in Britain before the 1997 elections.[62]

As I have argued, the MDC is a contradiction. While it was the struggle between 1996 and 1998 that gave birth to it, it was the very weakness of this movement and the political organisations of the working class that led to the party's failure to resist the pull of the middle class. Although it has been deflected from its founding purpose, it remains to many the crucial repository for their hope for social change. It is clear, however, that the MDC holds none of the answers to the poverty and misery crippling Zimbabwe. It too represents a hurdle that Zimbabwean workers must cross.[63]

Mass struggle is not only the answer for Zimbabwe. If the struggle is connected to Southern Africa's strongest link, the South African working class—which has repeatedly shaped political development in the region—then a radical alternative to the austerity and privatisation that have ravaged Africa can be found. But central to this is the need to build revolutionary socialist organisations that can give political clarity, practical strength and organisational strategy to the African working class. This has been the central objective and the acknowledged weakness of countless socialists and revolutionaries in Africa. As the Zimbabwean socialist Munyaradzi Gwisai has shown, the example of revolutionaries organising and participating in mass militant action is an invaluable lesson to all those who want to see the self emancipation of those crushed by Western imperialism (by Blair's 'initiatives') and local governments.[64] Conditions for this struggle are better today than they have ever been. The growth of an anti-capitalist movement is having an impact in the South African Anti-Privatisation Forums and in the general strike in August 2001. It is also touching Zimbabwean students and activists. If the hope that 'another world is possible' can be translated into socialist politics and organisation, and the development of a strong, independent rank and file movement in the region, then Southern Africa can again show the way to a better world.[65]

**Notes**

I would like to thank Andy Wynne, Miles Larmer, Dave Renton and Jocelyn Alexander for reading and commenting on an earlier version of this article.

1 *Business Day* (South Africa), 30 January 2002.

2 *The Guardian,* 10 January 2002.

3 *The Guardian*, 28 January 2002.

4 Ibid.

5 *The Daily Telegraph*, 27 August 2001; *The Observer* 22 April 2001.

6 *The Daily Telegraph*, 10 August 2001. News programmes are full of the catastrophe for white Zimbabwe. Jeremy Vine, a presenter on the British current affairs programme *Newsnight*, was determined to present the crisis as one harming principally black/white relations (28 January 2002).

7 Some see Mugabe as the leading figure in a rejuvenated pan-Africanism. He is keen to capitalise on this, speaking in Harlem, New York, in September 2000. See H Aidi, 'The Fire This Time: Pan-Africanism Comes to Harlem', http://www.africana.com/DailyArticles/index_20000921.htm. See also the absurd article by George Shire, suggesting that Mugabe is in fact the progressive choice in the elections: 'The Struggle For Our Land', *The Guardian*, 24 January 2002.

8 M Gwisai, 'Revolutionaries, Resistance and Crisis in Zimbabwe', in L Zeilig (ed), *Class Struggle and Resistance in Africa* (New Clarion Press: forthcoming 2002).

9 A Meldrum, *The Observer*, 30 September 2001.

10 See Global Witness, 'Zimbabwe's Resource Colonialism in the DRC', 26 August 2001, http://www.oneworld.org/globalwitness/press/bd_zimbabwe.htm

11 International Socialist Organisation activist Luke Kasuwanga. Unless otherwise indicated all quotations are taken from interviews conducted in London throughout July 2001.

12 P Alexander, 'Zimbabwean Workers, the MDC and the 2000 Election', *Review of African Political Economy* 85, pp385-387.

13 Cited ibid, p394.

14 M Gwisai, op cit. See P Bond, *Uneven Zimbabwe: A Study of Finance, Development, and Underdevelopment* (Trenton, 1998), ppxxiv-xxviii. It is important to remember that the picture of land ownership and control is constantly changing due to recent seizures. The extent of these seizures is impossible to quantify exactly. See the brilliant paper by J Alexander, 'Squatters, Veterans and the State in Zimbabwe', in A Hammer, B Raftopoulos and S Jensen (eds), *Unfinished Business: Rethinking Land, State and Citizenship in Zimbabwe* (Harare and Oxford, forthcoming 2002).

15 For a detailed study of land in Zimbabwe see J Matowanyika, 'The History of Land Use in Zimbabwe from 1900', available on the net, http://www.lead.org/lead/training/international/zimbabwe/1997/papers/d1matowan.html

16 C McGreal, 'The Trail from Lancaster House', *The Guardian*, 16 January 2002.

17 C van Onselen, *Chibharo: African Mine Labour in Southern Rhodesia 1900-1933* (London, 1976). See generally I Mandaza (ed), *Zimbabwe: A Political Economy of Transition 1980-86* (Dakar, 1986) and P Bond, op cit.

18 See the excellent illustrated history of the Zimbabwe trade union: B Raftopoulos and I Phimister (eds), *Keep on Knocking: A History of the Labour Movement in Zimbabwe 1900-1997* (Harare, 1997).

19 M Gwisai, op cit.

20 Cited in B Raftopoulos 'The Labour Movement in Zimbabwe: 1945-1965', in B Raftopoulos and I Phimister (eds), op cit, p65.

21 Cited ibid, p67.

22 Cited ibid, p68.

23 Ibid, p71.

24 Cited ibid, pp69-70.

25 A Astrow's excellent book looks at this process: *Zimbabwe: A Revolution That Lost its Way?* (London, 1983), p21.

26 A Callinicos and J Rogers, 'Southern Africa after Zimbabwe', *International Socialism* 9 (Summer 1980).

27 See A Astrow's excellent book, op cit, pp107-108.

28 The precise figure is still contested. It was subject to the ruling class tradition of a 'gentleman's agreement'.

29 Resettlement was quite successful in comparison to similar projects in other African countries. Productivity even outstripped the communal areas on a hectare for hectare basis. For those who experienced the resettlement it transformed their lives, but for the thousands left landless and poor it was undoubtedly a bitter disappointment. See B H Kinsey and H P Binswanger, *Characteristics and Performance of Settlement Programs: A Review* (Washington DC, 1993).

30 A cursory glance at Zimbabwe reveals the total lack of integration. It is typical across Africa today, even in countries that had no experience of settler communities. The image is identical to the popular conception of apartheid South Africa—rich white suburbs, with large green lawns watered by black staff and black security guards guarding palatial houses with swimming pools and

enormous gardens. These areas sit cheek by jowl with sprawling townships and terrible poverty. The lifestyles (and even the attitudes) of those who live like this have not changed substantially since independence.

31 See J Alexander, op cit, She argues that, up until February 2000, occupations were often popularly driven and the reaction of the government towards them was contradictory—similar to the situation in the early 1980s.

32 Cited in D Smith et al, *Mugabe* (Salisbury, 1981), p210.

33 It did not take years for bitterness to build up after independence. There were many who were disillusioned with Mugabe's moderate stand. The incident involving Edgar Tekere, a leading figure in the party and a close confidante of Mugabe, is illustrative. Only a year after independence he was implicated in an attack on a farmhouse and the death of a white farmer. After these events Mugabe, in the words of one commentator at the time, 'spiked the guns of his troublesome left wing'. Resentment amongst the left wing and thousands who had waited for victory and liberation was growing. See D Smith, op cit, pp209-218.

34 T Skalnes, *The Politics of Economic Reform in Zimbabwe* (London, 1995), p5.

35 See *Breaking the Silence, Building True Peace: A Report on the Disturbances in Matabeleland and the Midlands 1980-1988* (Harare, 1997). Also J Alexander, J McGregor and T Ranger, *Violence and Memory: One Hundred Years in the Dark Forests of Matabeleland* (London, 2000). Both these works detail these events and their impact on rural Matabeleland.

36 Department of Research and Planning, *Labour and Economy: Report of the National Trade Unions Survey, Zimbabwe*, volume one (Harare, 1984).

37 E Z Razemba, *The Political Economy of Zimbabwe: Impact of Structural Adjustment Programmes, 1980-1993* (Harare, 1994), pp89-91.

38 Bond, op cit, p150.

39 E Z Razemba, op cit, p131.

40 Skalnes makes this point: 'Chidzero was the one who steered the new economic philosophy through the cabinet.' T Skalnes, op cit, p131.

41 For an examination of the effects of this intervention see E Z Razemba, op cit.

42 P Jackson, 'The Role of the State in Business Development in Zimbabwe: The Case of the Textiles and Garments Sector', University of Birmingham. A summary of the paper can be found on the net: http://www.bham.ac.uk/IDD/activities/rog/paper13.htm

43 P Bond, op cit, p150.

44 Ibid, pp92-94.

45 T Skalnes, op cit, p141.

46 Cited in P Alexander, op cit, p386.

47 M Gwisai, op cit.

48 The strike also saw the active intervention of the International Socialist Organisation (ISO), the sister organisation in Zimbabwe of the Socialist Workers Party. Although at the time it had only 50 members, they were able to produce leaflets calling for indefinite action and had participated in the strikes in Harare and the second city, Bulawayo. As well as calling for the election of a strike committee to take the strike forward, they pressed for more militant action, including picketing government buildings.

49 Cited in P Alexander, op cit, p389.

50 It is important to be clear that the 'war veterans' are divided. While some support the government, others are aware of the cynicism of the new policy towards them.

51 See the government report: www.hrforumzim.com/genreps/foodriots98/food9801a.htm

52 Again the ISO helped to organise similar movements in other towns and produced a leaflet that called on others to join the struggle. The organisation's slogan 'Shinga Mushandi Shinga! Qina Msebenzi Qina!' ('Workers be resolute! Fight on!') has become the de facto motto of the trade union movement.

53 Chenjerai Hunzvi was a qualified doctor who had studied and lived in Eastern Europe. He was fluent in Polish, Romanian and French, and did not return to Zimbabwe until 1990, having left the country on a scholarship in the 1970s. See his obituary in *The Guardian*, 5 June 2001.

54 J Ihonvbere, *Economic Crisis, Civil Society and Democratization: T§he Case of Zambia* (Trenton, 1996).

55 ZANU-PF has stated that it intended to seize 8.5 million hectares of land before the presidential elections, which is the majority of land owned by white farmers.

56 Timothy Chitambure, interview July 2001.

57 See *Socialist Worker* (Zimbabwe), July-August 2001.

58 The MP was Munyaradzi Gwisai, a leading member of the ISO. See his chapter, op cit, and interview, 'A Worker's Voice', *Socialist Review*, September 2000.

59 This is certainly not the same as arguing that it is a vehicle for social change. The organisation is thoroughly under the grip of a right wing, neo-liberal agenda.

60 The title of his famous book. W Rodney, *How Europe Underdeveloped Africa* (London, 1988).

61 The government even established a rival trade union organisation, the Zimbabwe Federation of Trade Unions, which remains without members or affiliated unions.

62 Many of these observations were made to me by Miles Larmer after a recent visit to Zimbabwe.

63 It is important to emphasise the extent of this contradiction. In a recent interview with Collen Gwiyo, general secretary of the banking union, ZIBAWU, he stated that he did not think Eddie Cross, the right wing economic spokesperson for the MDC, would become the minister of finance, but that the post would go to a figure deemed more acceptable to workers. There is still the expectation, certainly among trade union bureaucrats, that the MDC may play a more progressive role in power.

64 M Gwisai, op cit.

65 See, for a Marxist account of the struggles that have gripped Africa, L Zeilig (ed), op cit.

# Pierre Bourdieu: voice of resistance

JIM WOLFREYS

The death of Pierre Bourdieu in January is a setback for the left both in France and internationally. A leading figure in French sociology since the 1960s, during the past decade Bourdieu played a major role in the backlash against the neo-liberal consensus among French intellectuals, firstly with the monumental collective work *The Weight of the World*, a collection of essays and interviews which exposed for a mass audience the brutal consequences of the unfettered market, and secondly as the active champion of the various groups and associations to emerge in the wake of the great public sector strike wave of December 1995. *The Weight of the World* was published in 1993 in the twilight years of the Mitterrand era. The intensification of social inequality and the various effects of job insecurity, unemployment and the flexibilisation of labour meant that for the first time since the war a generation had emerged whose conditions of work were inferior to those of its parents. The book laid bare, with an understated power, the way in which these changes shaped the everyday acts of individuals forced to count the cost in terms of fading hopes and shrunken lives. But if the failure of the Socialist Party to deliver social reform during the 1980s had bred confusion and despondency, by the early 1990s activists had begun to find ways of operating independently of the social democratic and trade union bureaucracy. *The Weight of the World* therefore chimed with people's experience, but also served as a justification for protest. Typical of the response it generated was that of a young teacher who, in a 1998 article for *Le Monde* about the strike he was involved in, wrote that those who affected not to understand the situation faced by those in deprived areas should go back and read Bourdieu's book.[1]

When unemployment hit the 3 million mark in the early 1990s, the full extent of social deprivation in France began to hit home, and small but significant groups of workers and students began to take action. As Robert Castel has noted, the protests of those affected were motivated not so much by the demand for 'always more' as the fear of 'always less'.[2] The burgeoning reaction against neo-liberalism eventually exploded in the form of three heady weeks of strikes and demonstrations against Gaullist plans to reform the social security system in November and December 1995. The most startling repercussions were political—within 18 months the mainstream right's utter dominance in parliament had crumbled, and by 1998 the fascist Front National had split.[3] But there was also a shift in the balance of power among French intellectuals. Since the mid-1970s a concerted attack had been waged not just on Marxist ideas but also on the relevance of any kind of political engagement by intellectuals, or indeed anyone. Once the prominent role of individuals who engaged with the Marxist tradition, like Sartre, Althusser and the historian Albert Soboul, had faded, French intellectual life in the 1980s was increasingly peopled by media-friendly figures like the historian Francois Furet, the sociologists Alain Touraine and Pierre Rosanvallon, and the journalist-philosopher Bernard-Henri Lévy. All shared a previous engagement with the left and a new-found desire to embrace moderation and consensus. Magazines like *Le Point* and *Le Nouvel Observateur*, along with journals like *L'Esprit* and *Le Débat*, gave them a platform, and influential think-tanks like the *Fondation Saint-Simon* were formed to propagate their ideas. 'Non-engagement', claimed the editor of *Le Débat*, 'was our flag'.[4] The slogan of the 1995 protests, '*Tous ensemble!*' ('All together!'), appeared to confound the consensus underpinning the new orthodoxy. When those linked to *L'Esprit* published a petition saluting the courage of Nicole Notat, the leader of the CFDT trade union federation whose craven attitude towards government cuts in social security had lost her the respect of a sizeable part of her own membership, Bourdieu stepped into the fray. He produced the final draft of a petition of intellectuals expressing support for the strikes. According to a colleague, Bourdieu felt that 'with the railway workers, he was defending a civilisation'.[5] A week later he addressed a public meeting of strikers, and condemned those intellectuals who were unable to understand the movement. 'This crisis,' he argued, 'is a historic opportunity for France and all those who refuse the new alternative—liberalism or barbarism'.[6]

Commentators frequently distinguish between Bourdieu the sociologist and Bourdieu the activist. Often this is to enable his opponents to bury the latter while praising the former. There is nevertheless a common thread which links his academic output and political activity, which is a preoccupation with how mechanisms of domination are reproduced. His first work on Algeria in the early 1960s, which examined the effect of colonisation and modernisation on traditional society and culture, looked at how individuals adapt to forms of domination, becoming acquiescent, if involuntary, participants in their own subjugation. The same applied to his subsequent influential analyses of the French education system. The book he produced with Jean-Claude Passeron, *The Inheritors*, crystallised many of the concerns with which Bourdieu would wrestle for the best part of the next four decades. In it he demonstrated how education, supposedly the means *par excellence* of social mobility, instead reproduced social inequality. Moreover, the individuals who ran the system were labouring under the illusion that they were overcoming the constraints of class or gender, while all the time conforming to attitudes and behaviour which perpetuated such divisions. How could the discrepancy between the apparent function of the education system and its role in maintaining inequality be overcome? Bourdieu and Passeron concluded that there was no alternative but to take the stated purpose of the system at face value if there was to be any hope that the actual function of education in society might eventually be displaced.

In subsequent works Bourdieu further developed his analysis of how those in power preserve their domination by means other than direct repression. Central to this process was the way in which inequalities of wealth and income appear in society to be not so much the products of economic injustice, as the natural consequence of disparities of ability, judgement or lifestyle. Domination was not imposed by one group of individuals on another but maintained indirectly, via institutions and practices which function with the complicity of the dominated. The key conceptual tool developed by Bourdieu to explain this complicity was the 'habitus', which mediates the relationship between human actors and society, producing patterns of behaviour whose limits are shaped by society's norms and implicitly, if unwittingly, accepted by individuals. As with the earlier work on education, then, the question remained—what solution could be offered? If individuals reproduced the structures of domination which enslaved them, how were they to break the circle? Although a similar question might be asked of Marxism—how is self emancipation possible if the dominant ideas in society are those of our rulers?—Bourdieu dismissed Marx's emphasis on workers' ability to consciously take control of their lives through the lived experience of class conflict as both voluntaristic, placing too much reliance on subjective consciousness, and deterministic, anticipating the 'maturing' of objective conditions.[7] While the prospect of liberation may have remained distant in Bourdieu's work, he did provide a series of impressive analyses which deployed the various conceptual tools he had developed over the years in rigorous and detailed explorations of his chosen fields of study, whether artistic production (*The Rules of Art*), education (*Reproduction in Education, Society and Culture*, with J-C Passeron), intellectual production (*Homo Academicus, Pascalian Meditations*) or, in perhaps his finest book, cultural consumption (*Distinction*).

In practical terms, although Bourdieu remained true to an essentially reformist outlook, the abandonment of reformism by French social democracy at a time when the welfare state was under attack led him to adopt a more radical stance. As chair of sociology at the prestigious Collège de France, Bourdieu's reputation and authority guaranteed maximum publicity for his interventions. Publications like *Acts of Resistance* demonstrate his commitment to polarising debate and bringing it to as wide an audience as possible. In this way he played a major role in ensuring that the technocratic 'experts' of the mainstream were not let off the hook. One of the constant themes of Bourdieu's work was the need for intellectuals (and their audience) to recognise the fact that they are social actors as well as observers. In *Reproduction* Bourdieu had criticised 'the infantry of all the avant-gardes, constantly scouring the horizon of modernity through fear of missing out on an ideological or theoretical revolution, ready to discern the latest addition to the "new classes", "new alienations" or "new contradictions".'[8] After 1995 many such figures, in particular those whose fame derived from their role as theoreticians of 'social movements', found they had been overtaken by the movement itself. Bourdieu did not let them forget it. In his speeches he lambasted the 'lackeys' of the establishment, while in a recent documentary he referred to sociologists who put themselves at the service of the state as 'scabs'.[9] The publishing house he had helped set up, *Liber—Raisons d'Agir*, produced a series of cheap, accessible books for the movement including *Les Nouveaux Chiens de Garde* (*The New Watchdogs*), a coruscating attack by Serge Halimi on the complicity between the media and the status quo, which addressed many of the themes taken up by Bourdieu himself in his 1996 book *Sur la Télévision*. Meanwhile, as a series of heterodox think-tanks, reviews and journals began to emerge, popular publications like the TV guide *Télérama* and the music and arts magazine *Les Incrockuptibles* started giving space over to Bourdieu and his collaborators, as did the more highbrow *Le Monde diplomatique*, which recast itself as an anti-globalisation publication with spectacular success. The discomfiture of those in the firing line was epitomised by the attempt of Alain Touraine to claw back some credibility by travelling to Chiapas to attend a forum with Subcomandante Marcos and the Zapatistas.[10] But the cosy certainties of their world had been severely shaken. Some of the signatories to the *Esprit* petition later tried to recant. In 1999 the *Fondation Saint-Simon*, the think-tank which spawned a thousand revisions, from Furet's distortions of the French Revolution to the report on France's 'social fracture' which gave Chirac his 1995 election slogan, folded.

'I was an angry young man,' Bourdieu told a conference organised last summer to discuss his work. 'I am an angry old man'.[11] His recent stance did not represent a break with his previous convictions, but the form in which they were expressed did become more direct and polemical. This was partly due to the manner in which the stakes were raised by the events of December 1995, but partly also due to the space opened up by the decline of social democracy for critical intellectuals, associations like ATTAC, independent trade unions, the far left and all the other components of the so called 'social movement'. The bitter sarcasm of a slogan painted on the walls of an Argentinian city during the recent wave of protests—'No more reality. We want promises'—underlines the extent to which mainstream politics across the globe are increasingly being reduced to the alternative, rejected by Bourdieu, of neo-liberalism or barbarism. After December 1995 Bourdieu gave his backing to a number of struggles, from the protests organised by immigrants denied residence papers to the wave of occupations by unemployed workers which swept France in 1997-1998 and, of course, the growing anti-capitalist movement in France and elsewhere. His own attempt to organise an 'Estates General of the European Social Movement', although it never really built up momentum, was part of an ongoing search for an alternative to existing social democratic parties which in France has found its most significant expression in the form of ATTAC, an organisation somewhere between an association and a political party. Those who fought alongside him as part of the anti-capitalist movement responded to the news of his death by stressing his unpretentious approach to activity, the fact that he could also be tough and critical with his support, and his contribution as a thinker and polemicist: 'He knew how to find the words for our fight'.[12] Some of his political opponents were predictably graceless in their comments, damning him with faint praise or choosing to attack the 'sectarianism' of his collaborators. Such reactions reflect a polarisation which Bourdieu had helped intensify, and the contours of a political struggle in which his contribution will be missed.

**Notes**

1 *Le Monde*, 28 March 1998.
2 R Castel, *Les Métamorphoses de la Question Sociale* (Paris, 1999), pp717.
3 See J Wolfreys, 'Class Struggles in France', *International Socialism* 84 (Autumn 1999).
4 P Nora, cited in J Duval, C Gaubert, F Lebaron, D Marchetti and F Pavis, *Le Décembre des Intellectuels Français* (Paris, 1998), pp47-48.
5 L Wacquant, *Le Monde*, 25 January 2002.

6 *Le Monde*, 14 December 1995.
7 For further comments on Bourdieu's relationship to Marxism see J Wolfreys, 'In Perspective: Pierre Bourdieu', *International Socialism* 87 (Summer 2000). For an excellent account of the development of his ideas see J Lane, *Pierre Bourdieu: A Critical Introduction* (London, 2000). On Bourdieu and the role of the engaged intellectual, see A Callinicos, 'Anthony Giddens or Pierre Bourdieu?', *New Left Review* 236 (July/August 1999).
8 P Bourdieu and J-C Passeron, *La Reproduction: Éléments Pour une Théorie du Système d'Enseignement* (Paris, 1970), p228.
9 P Carles (dir), *La Sociologie est un Sport Combat* (2001).
10 J Duval et al, op cit, p107.
11 *Le Temps*, 26 January 2002.
12 E Toussaint, *Le Nouvel Observateur*, 31 January 2002.

# Memoirs of a revolutionary

*A review of Susan Weissman,* ***Victor Serge: The Course Is Set On Hope*** *(Verso, 2001), £22*

RICHARD GREEMAN[1]

Victor Serge (né Kibalchich) was a French-language writer and international revolutionary whose activity spanned the first half of the 20th century. Born in 1890 in Brussels to a family of Russian revolutionary exiles, he became a professional militant and pamphleteer in his teens. His commitment to freedom and social justice evolved from involvement in the Belgian Socialist Young Guards through French anarchist individualism and Spanish anarcho-syndicalism to Russian Communism and its Left Opposition. A stateless exile and internationalist 'from birth', Serge was a participant-witness at crucial turning points in world revolutionary history, including the 'tragic bandits' of pre First World War French anarchism, the Barcelona syndicalist uprising of 1917, the Russian Civil War (he joined the Bolshevik Party in Petrograd in 1919), the failed German Revolution of 1923 (he was a Comintern publicist in Berlin), the Left Opposition's battle against Stalinism (he was expelled from the Bolshevik Party in 1928 for denoucing Stalin's betrayal of the Chinese Revolution), the fight against fascism and Stalinism in Spain (he was a fraternal member of the extreme left POUM), the Nazi occupation of France, and the exodus of revolutionary refugees to Mexico (where, as Weissman's research reveals, he was on the assassination list of the Soviet secret police, the NKVD).

Although Weissman's book attempts to span the full range of Serge's life, activities and ideas, the main subject of *The Course is Set on Hope* is Serge's analysis of Stalinism, a subject which Weissman handles with assurance, having devoted a 1991 doctoral dissertation and half a dozen overlapping published articles to it. Weissman bases her study largely on Serge's *Memoirs* and his *Russia Twenty Years After* (which she recently re-edited for Humanities Press).[2] She shows convincingly how Serge, while avoiding abstract theoretical arguments about 'degenerate' or 'deformed' workers' states, compiled large syntheses of statistical and anecdotal material to present a compelling picture of a Russian 'socialism' dominated by 10 percent of privileged bureaucrats and party bosses on the top, with a reserve army of about 16 percent of slave labourers in the camps on the bottom, and in between a vast majority of exploited, undernourished workers driven by police terror and deprived of any say over their conditions of labour. Serge described concretely the conditions of women, workers, students and peasants in the collective farms without spending much time speculating over whether the ruling bureaucracy that exploited them was a 'class' or a 'caste', an analysis he in any case considered premature.

Weissman, who apparently favours a 'bureaucratic collectivist' analysis, is somewhat uncomfortable with what she considers Serge's elusiveness and inconsistency on the question (especially since he occasionally wrote about 'state-capitalism' in his novels). Nor is she totally satisfied by Serge's 'sociological' explanation of Stalin's rise based on the votes of thousands of opportunists inducted into the Bolshevik Party after Lenin's death in 1924. On the other hand, she appreciates Serge's description of the 'chaos' of the 'plan' imposed from above by a Stalin lurching from one crisis to another. She also expounds Serge's explanation of the Moscow Trials, where the fake confessions of Zinoviev, Bukharin and other old Bolsheviks were obtained by a combination of psychological and physical torture, prior selection of defendants (the majority of Bolsheviks refused to confess and were shot in the cellars of the secret police), and 'party patriotism'. On this last point, she agrees with Serge's hindsight conclusion that excessive loyalty to an increasingly bureaucratic party hamstrung first Trotsky, who remained passive between 1923 and 1926, and later the Left Opposition, which out of party discipline (long after its expulsion!) denied itself the right to appeal to the non-party masses.

Serge's own claim to originality as an analyst of Stalinism was that he was apparently the first to describe (in 1933) this system as 'totalitarian' and compare it to the Nazi and fascist systems. However, as Weissman points out, Serge made it clear that Nazi totalitarianism stemmed from a failed socialist revolution and the inability of German capitalism to solve its problems through democratic means, whereas the origin of Stalinist totalitarianism was a proletarian revolution that had been hijacked by a party bureaucracy which was still forced to use, or rather misuse,

Marxist language in order to justify its rule.

Curiously, Weissman does not take this analysis one step further as Serge did both in his 1937 book and in his final essay on the subject, 'Thirty Years After the Russian Revolution'.[3] There, with astounding prescience, Serge suggested that the Soviet bureaucracy, an unstable formation driven by terror, would eventually be tempted to legitimise its privileges in property forms and to seek an alliance with the international capitalist bourgeoisie, as apparently happened after 1989. Serge also predicted that in such a case, the language of Marxism would inevitably be discredited in the eyes of the masses for a whole period (thus leaving them without the tools to comprehend their situation), and that the rise of nationalism among the vast Muslim populations of the Soviet Union would represent a serious reactionary threat—in 1947! Moreover, unlike other 'totalitarianism' theorists and Western Sovietologists who saw the Communist system as immune to change from within (thus justifying Cold War military containment of Communism), Serge saw the system as inherently unstable and in any case never doubted the continuing resistance of ordinary Russians, based on his own experience. ('Russia is More Full of Revolutionaries Than Ever' is the title of one of his essays).

Weissman's 'modest first examination of Serge's political, social, literary and economic writings on the Soviet Union'[4] is thus a welcome addition to Serge studies. However, like many enthusiasts and academics, she is somewhat less than modest about the importance of her particular topic. 'Serge's critique of Stalinism was the core of his life and work',[5] she states at the outset, and reiterates to 'analyse the nature of the social organism emerging in the USSR. This became his life's work';[6] and again, 'Serge spent the rest of his life trying to analyse and characterise the new social formation, to define its nature.' This myopic attitude gets her into trouble when she comes to deal with other aspects of Serge, who after all led a rich and adventurous life, thought deeply about many topics, and will probably be remembered as much for his achievements as a novelist as for anything else.

On the topic of literature, Weissman has this to say: 'Serge was first and foremost a political animal, and it was only when barred from political action that he turned to literary activity'.[7] 'Writing, for Serge, was something to do only when one was unable to fight.'

> *Serge wrote with a mission: to expose and analyse the significance of the rise of Stalinism. He worked continuously until he died, churning out novels, histories, pamphlets and polemics. In the years 1928 to 1936, while still in the Soviet Union, Serge wrote four* [sic] *novels, two* [sic] *short stories, and six works of history, politics and literary theory; he translated novels and poems*

*and seven volumes of history, politics, theory and memoirs. Considering the difficult circumstances under which Serge laboured, his prodigious output is extraordinary.*[8]

Indeed, *prodigiously* extraordinary, if measured in terms of literary Stakhanovism.[9] However, I wonder if Serge, who took literature seriously and considered himself 'in the line of the Russian novelists' (Tolstoy, Dostoyevsky, Turgenev, Korolenko), would be flattered by this purely quantitative appraisal of his fiction. On the qualitative side, although Weissman does sprinkle the words 'poetic' and 'lyrical' here and there in praise of Serge's writing (his style was actually understated and evocative), her aesthetic criterion is actually utilitarian. The most she has to say about Serge's complex and moving novel *Midnight in the Century* is that it is 'useful' for its account of certain theoretical discussions among exiled Left Oppositionsts.[10] She points to Serge's 'ability to see social reality clearly and honestly and write about it poetically' as if the poetry were the icing on a sociological cake. So much for aesthetics.

As for Serge's contribution to the debate on revolutionary literature, Weissman writes, 'Serge based his ideas on Trotsky's *Literature and Revolution*...in which Trotsky denied that a proletarian literature could exist' during the period of transition to socialism. (After that literature would become 'classless'.) But in 1932 Serge replied to Trotsky in his own *Literature and Revolution*[11] that 'the period of transition might be very long'. Whole generations of workers might live and struggle and die during that period, and 'they too would have their bards'. For this reason Serge defended the Proletcults and, from 1928 on, struck out on his own as the revolution's 'bard', bringing to life the comrades he had seen fall in the struggle and singing their heroism and their tragedy.[12]

Serge's mission was to 'speak for those who have no voice or whose voice has been silenced', to recreate the 'atmosphere' in which his characters struggle, to tell a truth he considered deeper than the economist's figures, the historian's facts and the theoretician's abstractions. His ultimate goal was 'to form the mind' and 'the character' of new generations, a task he considered essential in the face of the extermination of his own revolutionary generation by Stalin and Hitler.[13] I think he succeeded, judging from the number of people who have told me over the years of the profound effect reading Serge had on their personal and political outlook.

'Character' was an important notion for Serge, who wrote biographies of many revolutionaries, including book-length portraits of Lenin, Stalin, and Trotsky (the latter in collaboration with his widow, Natalia Sedova) in which he attempted to understand their psychology and show how these outstanding minds and personalities were forged by the revolutionary struggles of semi-feudal Russia. Although Weissman's book on Serge takes the form of a biography (and is praised as such on the jacket), she is not really comfortable with the notion and denigrates biographies, claiming they 'often fall into the genre of exposé...and speculation about emotional affairs designed to titillate the reader'.[14] Yet she titillates us on the first page of her preface, telling us breathlessly that one of the people she interviewed in preparing her biography 'was murdered just days before our appointment', but not telling us the person's name or the circumstances of this sensational crime.

Nonetheless, the best pages of *The Course Is Set On Hope* are precisely the most sensational ones, concerning assassination and espionage, where Weissman departs from summarising Serge's *Memoirs* and treats us to the fruits of some original biographical research she has done in the files of the FBI and the NKVD. Weissman leads us through the labyrinth of plot and counterplot among Stalin's 'killerocracy', using as a red thread Serge's involvement with NKVD defectors Walter Krivitsky, Alexander Barmine and 'Ignace Reiss' (who actually was murdered on the way to an appointment with Serge), but going far beyond Serge's role to explore the chilling world of assassins and agents-provocateurs.

Her principal quarry is the Stalinist agent 'Etienne' (Marc Zborovsky), who wormed his way into the Left Opposition in Paris, became the closest collaborator of Trotsky's son Leon Sedov (who died under mysterious circumstances in a Russian emigré hospital to which he was taken by Etienne), spied on all of Trotsky's correspondence, turned his followers against each other (for example, by casting suspicion on Serge), and fingered the Trotskyist militant Rudolf Klément (assassinated in Paris) and Reiss, who was about to break openly with the NKVD and join the Trotskyists when he was murdered. Like a bloodhound, Weissman followed Zborovsky's trail through the newly opened archives in Moscow, the files of the FBI and the US Senate committee (before which he testified in 1956) to San Francisco, where she camped on his doorstep demanding an interview (Zborovsky refused to open the door and shortly thereafter dropped dead).

Still, Weissman is ambivalent about whether she is writing an *analysis* of Serge's ideas on Stalinism or tracing their development biographically. The result is a narrative which, although it begins with his birth and ends with his death, jumps around in confusing ways, ignoring chronology in order to make general points. Sometimes she narrates the same incident twice. For example, the story of the suspicious murder by 'bandits' of Serge's Left Opposition comrade Chadayev in 1928 is told in full in two different places. Weissman deals with the Stalinists' brutal 1943 attack on Serge in Mexico City by introducing this story in the middle of her book (right after Serge's 1936 release from the gulag), in a section confusingly titled 'Part II. Another Exile and Two More: The Final Years'. She develops the story for several pages, and then drops it to pick up the thread of Serge's return to Europe in 1936. Eighty pages later, when she finally gets Serge to Mexico, she picks up the rest of the story, again at some length. But without continuity the reader gets lost in the details and loses the point.

Weissman's confusing anachronism can actually be quite misleading. For example, in order to demonstrate Serge's democratic credentials, she claims that 'he opposed one-party rule in 1918, and declared in 1923 that a coalition government, although fraught with risks, would be less dangerous than Stalin's secret police state'.[15] She repeats these claims later, stating, 'Serge consistently defended broad democratic rights both inside and outside the party, and had even suggested in 1923-1924 that a coalition government was preferable to the bureaucratic rule on its way to becoming the 'dictatorship of the secretariat and secret police'.[16] In fact, Serge proclaimed no such view either in 1918 (when he was a prisoner in a French concentration camp) or in 1923-1924 (when he was a Comintern journalist and undercover agent in Berlin and Vienna). Although he had private doubts about the dangers of bureaucracy and dictatorship early on, Serge first put forward these conclusions in hindsight, in 1937 (for example, in *Russia Twenty Years After*), when he tried to draw lessons from the the revolution's mistakes. To be charitable to Weissman, this is probably what she intends to say, but since she gives no references for these claims there is no way for a reader not to be misled.

Unfortunately, anachronism and confusion over dates is so prevalent that the reader never gets a sense of Serge's *development* as a man and a thinker, only a set of 'positions'. And since Serge's 'position' developed over time, Weissman inevitably ends up finding him inconsistent, for example on the essential issue of liberty and revolution. She writes:

> *Serge never succeeded in reconciling these contradictory stands. He clearly demonstrated the revolution was hemmed in from all sides: from within the anarchists, Socialist Revolutionaries (SRs), Mensheviks and Kadets, all opposed the Bolsheviks and formed part of the counter-revolution...along with the White generals...and the armies of 14 capitalist powers...* [Yet] *later Serge examined the measures taken out of necessity and theorised that certain of them* [for example, the Cheka secret police] *formed the foundation of Stalinist totalitarianism.*[17]

To begin with, Serge did not lump the Russian anarchists with the counter-revolutionaries, as Weissman does consistently in her study. (Nor does she quote any of Serge's writing when he was an anarchist.)

Moreover, she seems to ignore the central concept which guided Serge's conduct throughout his revolutionary career: the militant's 'double duty' to defend the revolution from *both* its external enemies (the counter-revolutionaries) and its inner enemies (intolerance and bureaucracy). Serge first discussed 'double duty' in print in *Literature and Revolution* (1932), and it may be his most original contribution to revolutionary morality. The problem, of course, is how to balance these two duties of criticism and support from inside a movement to which one gives critical support.

Serge's revolutionary career was just such a balancing act, and as such it is instructive when seen chronologically and in context. Serge was already a seasoned 29 year old anarchist militant when he arrived in Red Petrograd at the height of the civil war, and he was immediately shocked by the grim uniformity imposed on the press by the regime. How did he apply his concept of 'double duty'? As he wrote back to his friends and to anarchist journals in France, he saw no other group than the Communists effectively defending the fledgling Russian republic; and since he had come to Russia to defend it, he decided to join them as a libertarian, hoping for the day when he could successfully fight the Communists' authoritarianism. On two occasions Serge took up arms in defence of Petrograd against the White armies at the gate. He patrolled the city at night with a rifle invading people's appartments to hunt out counter-revolutionaries. He defended the Red Terror with his pen as well.

At the same time, privately, Serge used his personal connections with Gorky (who spoke directly to Lenin), with Zinoviev, and with many prominent Chekists, to intercede and save anarchist militants who had run foul of the regime. He attended Kropotkin's funeral, probably the last legal anarchist demonstration in Russia, and was the only Communist there (not counting menacing policemen). He met privately with the more trustworthy of the delegates who came from France, Italy and Spain to attend the early Congresses of the Comintern and the Profintern (the Red International of Labour Unions), opened their eyes to the realities of Moscow, and shared with them his doubts and misgivings about the revolution. These rather risky private initiations bore fruit. These comrades—revolutionary syndicalists like Rosmer, Ghezzi, Nin and Maurin, later Surrealists like Rosenthal and Naville—were at the core of the anti-Stalinist left in the 1920s and 1930s.

Serge's attitude toward the Communists' repression of the revolt of the Kronstadt sailors was a typical embodiment of his sense of 'double duty'. At the beginning he intervened personally, along with his anarchist father-in-law Russakov and the US anarchists Emma Goldman and Alexander Berkman, attempting to mediate the conflict between the government and the rebels (rather daring for a disciplined party member in the middle of a civil war). He criticised the brutal way the regime handled the affair: refusing to negotiate or listen to the sailors' quite justifiable demands and slandering them as 'counter-revolutionaries' commanded by a White general. In the end, however, with enemy battleships poised as the ice melted and with the island fortress of Kronstadt no longer defending Petrograd from the Whites, Serge reluctantly sided with the Communists in repressing the rebels, believing that the country was too exhausted to begin a 'third' revolution. Disgusted, he then left politics to form a short-lived anarchist farming comune and ultimately accepted a Comintern job in Berlin where he hoped to help bring to birth a new European revolution which would relieve Russia's isolation and revive the participatory, democratic side of socialism on an international scale.

Concerning what Weissman calls Serge's 'contradictory stand' about the Cheka leading to 'Stalinist totalitarianism', it is true that Serge, as we have seen, justified the Red Terror as a necessary defence against the White Terror, which he considered much more bloody since the counter-revolution must massacre large and numerous classes of people to triumph. (Weissman is excellent on this point in her discussion of the bloodbath of workers that followed the defeat of the peacefully-elected Finnish Socialist Republic, abandoned by the Bolsheviks at Brest-Litovsk). Serge also concluded that the Cheka was 'Lenin's biggest mistake'.

What Weissman fails to tell her readers is what Serge thought Lenin *should have done* (and what future revolutions should do). Serge thought that the counter-revolutionaries, who were numerous and dangerous behind the Red lines, could have been hunted out and brought before mass tribunals. There suspects could at least hear the charges against them, face their accusers, contradict witnesses, speak in their defence and, if found guilty, be jailed or shot. I remember this happening in Havana during the first days of the Cuban Revolution, and although the spectacle was at times quite horrifiying and there were probably some injustices done, these mass trials were effective and purifying. On the other hand, the Cheka secret police method of condemning a suspect to death on the basis of written reports, without seeing or hearing him or her or permitting any defence, could only lead to the creation of an all-powerful and totally paranoid inquisition which could and did turn on the revolution and devour it. One may not agree with Serge's solutions, but it is perhaps misleading to contend, as Weissman does, that he was inconsistent and had no solution.

Finally, Serge did away with the false problem of 'Bolshevism leading to Stalinism' as follows: 'It is often said that "the germ of all Stalinism was in Bolshevism at its beginning". Well, I have no objection.

Only, Bolshevism also contained many other germs, a mass of other germs… To judge the living man by the death germs which the autopsy reveals in a corpse—and which he may have carried in him since his birth—is that very sensible?'[18]

Serge's interpretation of his double duty was thus complex, evolving through time and depending on concrete circumstances. Although one could argue with the politics of any one of Serge's judgements, I find his attitude of double duty as a whole exemplary, in the sense of setting an example we can all try to follow. On the other hand, our ability to understand Serge's specific 'positions' depends on our understanding of the context: *where* Serge wrote what he wrote (in an official party publication, a letter to a comrade, a polemic, a novel, his *Notebooks*, his *Memoirs*) and *when* he wrote it (at the time or in retrospect). Unfortunately, context is not Weissman's strong suit, what with her attitude towards biography and her aversion to chronology. Only readers thoroughly conversant with Serge and Bolshevik historiography can follow her arguments, whereas new readers would be better advised to read Serge's *Memoirs* and *Russia Twenty Years After*, on which most of Weissman's interpretation is based.

Serge ended his *Memoirs of a Revolutionary 1901-1941* with his 1941 arrival in Mexico, where he died in 1947, and so readers familiar with Serge look forward to an account of his life, his struggles, and his ideas during those final years. Unfortunately, Weissman devotes a scant 15 pages to the Mexican years and tells us precious little about Serge's Mexican writings (mostly unpublished), which were prolific on every subject from the military conduct of the Second World War and the problem of Stalinism in post-war Europe to literature, psychoanalysis, Mexican anthropology, the atom bomb, and the role of human intelligence in history (not counting the three novels he completed in Mexico). Weissman summarises them as follows: 'In the end Serge left hundreds of essays, all of which deserve publication. His thoughts expressed throughout were broadly similar'.[19]

I am not sure all these essays are equally deserving of publication, since many of them (for example, on Russian, Japanese and Nazi military tactics in 1943) are quite dated. But the thoughts they expressed during this period of re-examination and revision were not 'broadly similar', and they do deserve to be read and analysed by Serge scholars. Unfortunately Weissman's book refers (glancingly) to only three of the manuscripts Serge left in what she refers to vaguely and inaccurately as the 'Serge archive, Mexico'. Let me state that there is no 'Serge archive' in Mexico. In 1996 Serge's son Vlady Kibalchich and I, after searching for years for a safe place to deposit Victor's posthumous papers, found a home for them at the Beinecke Rare Book and Manuscript Library of Yale University. The catalogue of the Victor Serge collection there is available online[20] and runs to 77 pages: rich fodder for future Serge scholars, but unfindable from Weissman's bibliography. Moreover, most of Serge's posthumous manuscripts (like his other writings) are in French, which is apparently a problem for Weissman.

Weissman does discuss some of Serge's Mexican-period writings, but (with the three exceptions mentioned above) mostly on the basis of published works available in English or Spanish translation (including John Manson's wonderful unpublished translations of Serge's *Notebooks*, available on line at http://www.victorserge.net). Her rare attempts at coping with Serge's French (the English version of the *Memoirs* being abridged) are hopeless. She has the newly liberated Serge 'worried' that he'll 'end up full of resentment' when the French text makes it clear that he was worried that his French friends would *think* he had arrived from Russia 'full of rancour'.[21] She has him say that 'political deportation is *never* ended because of firm convictions' (which makes little sense) when the French text means that Oppositionists who stick firmly to their convictions (as opposed to 'capitulators') never get released.[22]

Weissman is right on the mark to insist, as she does, that Serge never abandoned socialism and defended the historical justice of the October Revolution to the very end. This point is essential, since, as Weissman shows, his willingness to publish articles (for money—he was poor) in right social democrat papers like the *New Leader* and a compromising personal letter sent to Malraux in the hope of getting help to return to Europe allowed his detractors to spread the rumor of his 'deathbed conversion' to anti-socialism. She has done a yeoman's service in publishing Serge's 'Thirty Years After the Russian Revolution', written the month before he died, staunchly defending the Bolsheviks' role in 1917 and pointing to the bankruptcy of conservatism, Christianity and liberalism, which did nothing to prevent fascism.

On the other hand, in his final years Serge was searching for new answers in a rapidly changing world, which got him more or less expelled from the rigidly 'Marxist' exile group of Pivert, Gironella, and Malaquais (not Malaquaise, as Weissman writes) who were convinced that the Second World War would be followed by a new edition of 1917. Serge's posthumous manuscripts, many of which were probably not intended for publication, explore a variety of solutions to the problem of socialism and democracy in a world economy he saw as increasingly 'collectivist', whether nominally capitalist or Communist. Far from being 'broadly similar', Serge's thoughts need to be sorted out and analysed (especially now that photocopies of his manuscripts are available from Yale). Weissman takes a few shots at analysing some of the bits that have been translated, but lacks a coherent overview. She concludes, 'Serge thought that the new [post Second World War] Europe would be totalitarian and fascistic'.[23] Yet two pages later she declares, 'Serge was certain that socialism would ultimately win, and that it would first come in Europe, because Stalinism was inherently a weak system, even though he considered it more powerful and more dangerous than capitalism.' Right.

**Notes**

1 Richard Greeman (rgreeman@laposte.net) has translated four of Serge's novels into English and written numerous literary and political articles on Serge. He is secretary of the International Victor Serge Foundation and Serge's literary executor. He is based in France.
2 See 'Appendix: Recent works in English by or about Victor Serge' at the end of this article.
3 Written in 1947 and published for the first time in appendix to Weissman's edition of *Russia Twenty Years After* (London, 1996).
4 S Weissman, *The Course Is Set On Hope* (London, 2001), pxii.
5 Ibid, p6.
6 Ibid.
7 Ibid, p67.
8 Ibid, p111.
9 On the other hand, Serge did translate, albeit for money, Henriette Chaguinian's *Hydrocentrale* (Paris, 1933), that paean to the Five Year Plan.
10 S Weissman, op cit, p152.
11 V Serge, *Litterature et Révolution* (Paris, 1933, 1976 and 1978). Serge also wrote a regular chronicle of Soviet literary and intellectual life in the 1920s for the French review *Clarté*, edited by Henri Barbusse.
12 Although Serge dedicated a novel to Trotsky, the old man (who kept up with French fiction and wrote articles about Malraux, Malaquais and Céline) never bothered to read it. See R Greeman, 'Did Trotsky Read Serge?' in *Revolutionary History*, vol 7, no 2 (1999), special issue on 'Culture and Revolution in the Thought of Leon Trotsky'.
13 For further reading, see R Greeman, 'Victor Serge and the Novel of Revolution' in S Weissman (ed), *The Ideas of Victor Serge: A Life as a Work of Art* (Glasgow, 1999).
14 S Weissman, *The Course Is Set On Hope*, op cit, p7.
15 Ibid, p4.
16 Ibid, p119.
17 Ibid, p28.
18 V Serge, 'Reply to Ciliga', *New International*, February 1939. Quoted ibid, p324.
19 Ibid, p170.
20 http://webtext.library.yale.edu/xml2html/beinecke.SERGE.con.html#a3
21 S Weissman, *The Course Is Set on Hope*, op cit, p194.
22 Ibid, p164.
23 Ibid, p273.

**Appendix: Recent works in English by or about Victor Serge**

1992 Victor Serge, *The Case of Comrade Tulayev*, translated by Willard Trask (Journeyman Press/Pluto Press, London).
1992 Bill Marshall, *Victor Serge: The Uses of Dissent* (Berg, New York and Oxford).

1994 David Cotterill (ed), *The Serge-Trotsky Papers: Correspondence and Other Writings Between Victor Serge and Leon Trotsky* (Pluto Press, London and Boulder, Colorado). Includes essays by David Cotterill, Philip Spencer and Susan Weissman.

1994 *Revolutionary History*, vol 5, no 3, *Victor Serge: The Century of the Unexpected. Essays on Revolution and Counter-Revolution* (Socialist Platform Ltd, London).

1996 Victor Serge, *Russia Twenty Years After* (includes Serge's previously unpublished 'Thirty Years After the Russian Revolution'), translated with an introduction by Max Shachtman; new edition prepared with introductory essay by Susan Weissman (Humanities Press, London).

1997 Susan Weissman (ed), *The Ideas of Victor Serge: A Life as a Work of Art* (Critique Books, Glasgow).

1997 Victor Serge, *Revolution in Danger: Writings from Russia 1919-1921*, translated with an introduction by Ian Birchall (Redwords, London).

2000 Victor Serge, *Witness To the German Revolution*, translated with an Introduction by Ian Birchall (Redwords, London).

2001 Susan Weissman, *Victor Serge, The Course Is Set On Hope* (Verso, New York and London).

2001 Victor Serge, *Mémoires d'un Révolutionnaire et Autres Écrits Politiques 1908-1947* (Robert Laffont, Paris).

2002 *Victor Serge: Writer and Revolutionary*, website hosted by John Eden, richly illustrated by drawings and photos, includes excellent introductions to Serge's life and work, previously unpublished translations of Serge's *Notebooks*, and short essays: www.victorserge.net

2002 Richard Greeman's website (under construction) includes a dozen of his literary, political and biographical studies of Victor Serge from the 1960s up to today.

# The seeds of national liberation

*A review of Jeremy Smith,* ***The Bolsheviks and the National Question, 1917-1923*** *(Macmillan, 1999), £45*

DAVE CROUCH

About the time that the Soviet Union ceased to be a union ten years ago, historians became more interested in the origins of the forces tearing apart the world's largest state. How successful had the Bolsheviks been in resolving national tensions? Was there ever any hope that the USSR could survive as a stable multinational unit? Or were the seeds of its collapse present from the very start? What was the significance of disagreements among the Bolsheviks, in particular Lenin and Stalin, over the national question? After a decade that has seen appalling massacres of one national group by another in Yugoslavia, Rwanda, Kurdistan and East Timor, and during which governments like Tony Blair's have resorted to racist vilification of immigrants and asylum seekers, these questions have lost none of their pertinence.

For almost 50 years the standard work on this aspect of Soviet history has been Richard Pipes's *The Formation of the Soviet Union.* Pipes analysed vast quantities of Russian language literature from this period, and his book is still a valuable reference. But Pipes was starting out on a career as the foremost Cold War historian of Russia. His thesis was that Lenin's slogan of 'the right of nations to self determination' was nothing but a bait with which to lure the non-Russian peoples, 'a tactical device intended to win over the minorities'.[1] As soon as the regime felt sufficiently stable, according to Pipes, it moved to reconquer the borderlands and renege on its promises to the minorities. The formation of the Soviet Union in December 1922 was a decisive turning point in the resurrection of the Russian Empire. Pipes takes the extreme Russian chauvinism of the late Stalin period and reads it straight back to October 1917.

Nonetheless, the book retains an element of ambiguity. Reviewing Lenin's attack on Stalin in his 'testament', Pipes goes as far as to say that, had Lenin lived, his 'conciliatory attitude to dissident nationalism in the republics' would have meant that 'the final structure of the Soviet Union would have been quite different from that which Stalin ultimately gave it'.[2] A similar observation led Moshe Lewin in *Lenin's Last Struggle* to argue that Lenin's dispute with Stalin over the national question in 1922 was evidence of a deep divide between the libertarian goals of the Bolshevik Revolution and conservative, Stalinist reaction.[3]

Pipes's book concentrates almost exclusively on the political aspects of Bolshevik national policy, to the exclusion of culture and economics. French historian Hélène Carrère d'Encausse attempted to fill this gap, and it is significant that she rejects the Machiavellian interpretation prefered by Pipes. For Carrère d'Encausse, Lenin was neither a chauvinist nor an imperialist—his political principles were 'cogent and consistent', and in its early years the Bolshevik regime made genuine attempts to restore national rights and atone for the crimes of Tsarist colonialism.[4]

But if his intentions were good, Lenin's theories did not survive the test of concrete events: 'His earlier convictions crumbled in the face of a reality that could not be ignored.' Like Pipes, Carrère d'Encausse sees a contradiction between Lenin's centralism, on the one hand, and his defence of national rights on the other—in the end centralism was inevitably dominant.[5]

By shifting the focus to cultural and economic policy, however, Carrère d'Encausse began to reveal a picture very different from the straightforward imperialist conquest proposed by Pipes. More recent scholars have also been impressed by Bolshevik achievements in the national sphere in the 1920s. Yuri Slezkine, Russian specialist at the University of California, Berkeley, for example, argues that 'Soviet nationality policy was devised and carried out by [non-Russian] nationalists', while Harvard historian Terry Martin characterises the USSR as an 'affirmative action empire'.[6] This history was hidden from Russians themselves: 'The fact that the Soviets covered up the extent of pre-Stalinist nation-building and its anti-Russian thrust proves how politically volatile party leaders considered the rediscovery of what the 1920s were really like'.[7]

Despite the fact that Stalin, as Commissar for Nationalities, was the government minister responsible for national policy until 1923, his biographers (with the exception of Trotsky) are also oddly silent over the Bolsheviks' record on the national question. One historian calls this 'the myopia of professional Sovietology regarding the nationality question'.[8]

It is in this context that Jeremy Smith's book *The Bolsheviks and the National Question, 1917-1923* is a welcome contribution to rediscovering the Leninist legacy in this sphere. Based on copious archive research, Smith sets out to challenge many of Pipes's assumptions. This review will draw on his findings to help paint a broad picture of Bolshevik national policy after the revolution. It will then briefly examine his more important and controversial conclusions.

## Autonomy and independence

The Tsarist Empire stretched from Finland, the Baltic states and Ukraine through the Caucasus and Central Asia to the nomadic tribes of the far north. Imperial conquest had created a multinational state in which Russians made up just 43 percent of the population. National oppression of the non-Russian peoples was extreme, which gave the national question a gigantic explosive force. For Lenin this was the second most important issue for Marxists after the agrarian question.[9]

Towards the end of the First World War there were spectacular examples of the revolutionary potential of movements demanding national rights, evidenced in Trotsky's words that their nationalism was 'the outer shell of an immature Bolshevism'.[10] In the summer of 1916 the Kazak-Kyrgyz revolt against conscription was a massive and violent expression of popular dissatisfaction with the Tsarist regime. In May 1917 Russian Muslims became the first in the world to vote to free women from the restrictions to which they had traditionally been subjected in Islamic societies. In Kiev and several other Ukrainian cities nationalists aided the Bolsheviks in overthrowing the Provisional Government in October.[11]

But across the empire Russians were feared as colonisers and oppressors. So how was the new Soviet government to establish relations of trust with the non-Russian peoples?

In its Declaration of Rights the new government invited each nation in Russia 'to decide independently at its own plenipotentiary Soviet Congress whether and on what basis to participate' in federal government. The constitution adopted in July 1918 clarified that district soviets 'distinguished by a particular way of life and national composition' could come together and choose whether to enter the Russian Socialist Federative Soviet Republic (RSFSR).[12]

While those arrangements were being worked out, refined and formalised, national minorities enjoyed representation in central government and a certain amount of decision-making power through the newly created People's Commissariat of Nationality Affairs, or 'Narkomnats' for short. Here national representatives could examine central decrees, and take their comments and proposals directly to the government. Narkomnats therefore had a dual role—as an executive of central government on the one hand, and as a representative organ for the minorities on the other.

Narkomnats included subordinate commissariats for each of the main non-Russian national minorities. Smith comments:

> *Organised in a fairly ad hoc manner, left largely to their own devices by the higher organs of Soviet power while only under the loose supervision of the Narkomnats collegium, and frequently staffed by nationalists who had come over late to the Bolsheviks, there was considerable scope for these departments to play a major role in the evolution of national policy. They were to emerge as the political leaderships of a major portion of the Soviet population which were to spearhead the drive to national autonomy.*[13]

From 1917 to 1923 some 17 autonomous regions and republics were established within the Russian federation, and five independent republics outside it. The success of autonomy depended on placing authority in the hands of representatives of native peoples. But the regime faced an immediate problem—most national minorities were under-represented in the Communist Party and the soviets. Outside the Russian heartland the soviets were for the most part overwhelmingly Russian in composition and often exhibited racist hostility to the native populations. Native leaders were on the whole politically inexperienced and usually came from one of two extremes—conservative-religious or radical-nationalist, neither of which fitted comfortably with Bolshevik aspirations. Two possible courses of action offered themselves to resolve these contradictions—allow the Russian-dominated soviets to govern in the name of the national minorities, with strong supervision by Moscow to ensure a correct approach to the national question, or grant the national leaderships authority above that of the soviets, within negotiated limits.[14] The first approach is characterised by Turkestan, the second by Bashkiria.

In Turkestan—a vast south eastern territory bordering Afghanistan, Iran, China and Mongolia—national territorial autonomy was imposed by Moscow in a move explicitly designed to support native Muslims against the chauvinism of the Russian colonists. In many of the outlying parts of the empire Bolshevik organisation in October 1917 was virtually non-existent. In December 1917 the Bolshevik cell in Tashkent, capital of Turkestan, numbered just 64. Moreover, the small numbers of workers in these areas were often Russians deeply imbued with colonial attitudes. For them the Bolshevik slogan of proletarian dictatorship could be conveniently employed against the overwhelmingly rural native population. As a result, large numbers of colonists declared for the Bolsheviks in Turkestan after October and expressly excluded Muslims from the organs of Soviet power. According to a Bolshevik observer at the time, Soviet power in Tashkent in 1917 and early 1918 was largely in the hands of 'adventurers, careerists and plain criminal elements' determined to preserve the privileged position enjoyed by the Russian settlers.[15]

This led to vigorous intervention by the Bolshevik leadership to redress the situation—an 'extraordinary commissar' and other leading cadres were dispatched to sort out the chauvinists. In Smith's words, in spring 1918 'autonomy was fairly forced down the throat of Turkestan by Moscow' as a first step towards undermining the colonists. Turkestan was then cut off from Moscow by the civil war, after which Lenin once again intervened decisively to smash the Russian chauvinists.[16]

By contrast, in Bashkiria—a small territory in the western Urals—national feeling among the local population was more developed, and Bolshevik policy concentrated on wooing local nationalists and granting them widespread powers. Native leader Zeki Validov and his Bashkir National Council sided with the Whites at the start of the civil war. But Admiral Kolchak's hostility to the Bashkirs led Validov in February 1919 to bring his forces—6,500 men—over to the Reds, shifting the strategic situation on this part of the front decisively in favour of the Bolsheviks. In return Moscow negotiated the creation of a Bashkir Autonomous Soviet Republic. This was to have full power over the region—excluding major economic installations such as railways, factories and mines—its own armed forces (subordinate to the Red Army command) and a full amnesty for the Bashkir leaders, who governed the republic through the Bashkir Revolutionary Committee or Bashrevkom.

From the start, however, there was friction between the Bashrevkom and local Bolsheviks: 'It was generally accepted that, if it had not been for the influence of Moscow, local Bolsheviks would have done away with Bashkir autonomy altogether'.[17] In March 1920 Trotsky held several conferences in the Bashkir capital, Ufa, at which he condemned local Bolshevik interference in Bashkir affairs and backed the Bashrevkom.

With power in the hands of the Bashkir nationalists, however, there was a danger that a crisis of relations between Ufa and Moscow could lead to a Bashkir counter-revolution. Despite vigorous intervention from the centre, local Russian Communists continued to cause problems, and there was mounting concern in Moscow over the possible military implications. In the summer of 1920 these fears led Moscow to curtail Bashkir autonomy, which in turn provoked a fierce Bashkir revolt.

Nonetheless, the creation of the Bashkir republic firmly established the principle of autonomy for the national minorities of Russia. From 1920 to 1922 a string of new autonomous republics and regions were established in the Russian Federation for the Karelian, Chuvash, Kyrgyz, Tartar, Votiak, Kalmyk, Mari and North Caucasian peoples. Smith notes:

> *The creation of autonomous territories was usually accompanied by extensive research and discussion of the status of the nationalities involved. This was particularly the case with the lesser known groups whose definition as a distinct national group was not fully established, such as the Yakuts.*[18]

Of the eight autonomous republics in existence by the end of 1922, all except one had non-Russian populations that were predominantly Muslim—evidence that the Bolsheviks were particularly sensitive to the demands of Muslim peoples, who had suffered appalling treatment under the Tsars. Moscow was also acutely aware of the international impact of its national policies on the anti-colonial movements in the East, and wanted to be seen to be firmly on the side of the colonies in their struggle against European imperialism.[19]

Undermining local Russian chauvinism was a major factor in Moscow's encouragement of territorial autonomy. In each case, however, concrete material and subjective factors shaped relations between centre and periphery. For example, when in 1920 a keen, experienced and energetic Finnish comrade arrived in Moscow, convinced of the need for Karelian autonomy, that was sufficient for Lenin to give it the go-ahead. Smith's detailed discussion of the autonomous regions of Karabakh, Nakhichevan and Zangezur in Azerbaijan and Armenia, however, shows how complex the political equation could be. Factors included a recent history of racial massacres, diplomatic relations with Turkey, the ripening revolution in Armenia, economic considerations, the international situation, and the need to create beacons for Muslim peoples of the East.[20]

Establishing republics meant long and frequently contentious discussions over borders, in particular in the case of nomadic peoples such as the Kyrgyz-Kazaks. The separation of the Kyrgyz Autonomous Soviet Socialist Republic (the basis for present day Kazakstan) from Turkestan in August 1920 was the first move towards dividing the population of Central Asia into major national groups, each with its own language and territory. This process led in 1924 to the end of Turkestan and the establishment of Uzbek, Turkmen, Tajik and Kyrgyz autonomy.

Several authors have accused the Bolsheviks of artificially separating the peoples of Central Asia in a deliberate policy of divide and rule aimed at undermining pan-Islamic and pan-Turkic aspirations in the region.[21] Smith notes, however, that ideas of Islamic or Turkic unity had little influence outside intellectual circles. Moreover, his discussion makes clear that the 1924 delimitation was 'approached in a thoroughly scientific manner', the result of work on language and culture that began immediately after the revolution and applied equally to small native populations who posed no threat to Bolshevik rule. Indeed, rather than building up Slav unity—as might have been expected if the Bolsheviks had really perceived a threat from Islam—Moscow went to great lengths to establish a Belorussian national identity distinct from Russia. In 1919 it even acknowledged nationalists' nostalgia for the Grand Duchy of Lithuania by fusing the Belorussian Soviet Republic with the Lithuanian. This brief experiment in Belorussian-Lithuanian unity was brought to an end by the Polish invasion a few months later.[22]

Fledgling national states were further strengthened by Narkomnats' policy of encouraging the victims of Tsarist deportations, as well as refugees from war and famine, to settle in areas where their presence would bolster the titular peoples. A concomitant to this policy of voluntary migration were measures to forcibly remove Russian and other Slav colonists from the lands they had seized. In the North Caucasus the local population, with Bolshevik support, conducted a bitter campaign to evict 65,000 Cossack settlers, and turn over their land, livestock and belongings to the local Chechens and Ingush. As Pipes notes, this became the cornerstone of Bolshevik policy in the region for many years to come: 'It accounted for the loyalty shown by the Chechen and Ingush toward the Communists during the civil war'.[23]

In the Crimea and Central Asia, however, the natives were not strong enough to eject the Russian kulaks (wealthy peasants) without support from the central Russian state. In March 1921 the Politburo in Moscow resolved to evict troublesome Russian settlers from Turkestan, and pursue a more general policy of reversing colonisations and removing Russian kulaks from the region. Owing to famine and the political dangers inherent in the policy, forced evictions were fairly limited. In 1921-1922, for example, 7,000 native families were resettled onto former kulak land in Turkestan. Smith is at pains to point out that, unlike Stalin's mass deportation in the 1930s and 1940s, these compulsory migrations were not punitive of nations as a whole, but were seen as a means of righting past wrongs and promoting national peace in the long term.[24]

The Bolsheviks also began to redress the relative economic backwardness of Russia's borderlands:

> *The Soviets embarked on a massive programme of industrial development in the non-Russian areas, including the movement of whole enterprises from the central Russian region. Thus, according to Soviet sources, in Central Asia between 1918 and 1923 the following measures were taken: in 1918 50 million roubles were earmarked for construction work in the Golodniy steppe and 502 million for the restoration of the cotton industry in Turkestan; in 1922 a stationery and textile factory and a leather and soap works were moved to Bukhara, and a stationery and cellulose plant to Turkestan; two large factories from the Moscow region were also moved to Turkestan; in*

> *1918 a new soda plant was erected in Tashkent, and in 1919 a metalworking plant, a mechanical-transport plant and a foundry were also built... These projects were disproportionate to the general level of industrial investment in the RSFSR for this period.*[25]

One obvious effect of this policy of 'urbanising nations' was to boost the number of workers in favour of native peoples and away from the Russians, who predominated almost everywhere before the revolution. Thus, for example, before 1914 Ukrainians in industry were a small minority, but by the end of the 1920s they nearly equalled the Russians—41 percent and 42 percent of waged workers respectively.[26]

## National Communist leaderships

The existence of autonomous national territories could not continue without friction as long as political and administrative leadership remained in the hands of Russians. Events in Turkestan demonstrated what this could lead to, while Bashkiria showed the dangers of entrusting nationalists with power. Outside the Russian heartlands the Bolsheviks were generally weak, and therefore the need to recruit 'natives' to the Soviet state apparatus and to build non-Russian national leaderships became a recurrent theme in Bolshevik statements on the national question, especially after 1919. This was the policy of *korenizatsiia*, or 'indigenisation'. Smith demonstrates that the Bolsheviks pursued 'a deliberate long term strategy of placing political and especially cultural leadership in the hands of local non-Russians'.[27]

The Jewish socialist parties were among the first to indicate their willingness to work in co-operation with the Bolsheviks and move towards full unity with them. Although at first he opposed separate Jewish organisation within the Bolshevik Party, in January 1918 Lenin became concerned at the distance between the assimilated minority of Jews in the Russian Communist Party and the mass of non-assimilated Jews. Thus the Jewish Section of the Russian CP was established for Yiddish speakers for whom language was a barrier to active party membership.[28]

Although Western Jewish historians concentrate on the role of the pogroms in driving Jews over to the Bolsheviks, Smith points out that there were also many positive reasons for Jewish people to become Bolsheviks. For example, the Jewish socialist organisations, such as Paole Zion and the Bund, continued to operate openly. The Jewish Section concentrated its criticisms on the Zionist and right wing Jewish parties, not the Jewish socialists—in sharp contrast with the Bolsheviks' attitudes to the Russian socialist parties.[29]

Non-Bolshevik Jews played a major role in Narkomnats. Of the six-member collegium of the Jewish Commissariat of Narkomnats, only one was a Bolshevik. At a conference of the Jewish Commissariat and the Jewish Section in 1918 nearly half the delegates were non-Bolshevik Yiddish educationalists. Of 15 central committee members of the Bund in April 1917, seven joined the Communists and by 1920 two were on the Central Bureau of the Jewish Section. In Ukraine the Bund split and the left faction joined the Communist Party of Ukraine (CPU) in 1919, where 'it dominated the new Jewish sections'. Smith notes that 'of the early national communists, the Jews remained in positions of importance the longest'.[30]

In Ukraine the Bolsheviks were very short of native cadre. Disagreements over the national and agrarian questions, combined with the intensity of the civil war in Ukraine, had led to splits within the Bolsheviks and major conflict with Ukrainian nationalists, causing Lenin to demand a sharp change in policy in 1919. The Ukrainian Bolsheviks, however, had marched side by side with nationalists in 1917, and the latter had helped them overthrow the Provisional Government in Ukraine.[31] In 1918 and 1919 the peasant armies of the Ukrainian anarchist leaders Makhno and Hrihoriev fought alongside the Reds.

The *Borotbists* were the Ukrainian equivalent of the Left Socialist Revolutionaries in Russia—a peasant party which had backed the October Revolution. A large section of the *Borotbists* were more than ready to lend their support to the Bolsheviks, arguing that there was more to unite the two parties than divide them. Highly confident of their legitimacy as a genuinely Ukrainian organisation, in April 1919 the *Borotbists* applied for separate membership of the Comintern, and asserted their claim to being the leading party of the Ukrainian Revolution. In March 1919 the Kiev *Borotbists* called on their central committee to apply to join the CPU, and later that month their congress voted for merger. After long and intense negotiations with the *Borotbists,* the CPU voted to accept the merger in March 1920—4,000 out of 5,000 *Borotbists* joined the CPU, and two were appointed to the central committee.[32]

Smith compares the policy here with the disaster of the Bashrevkom. Co-opting the *Borotbists*, whose policies on national culture dovetailed with the Bolsheviks', was a middle way between the nationalists and Russian chauvinists.

In Central Asia the Bolsheviks managed to make alliances against the Whites with a range of nationalist groups: the Kazak pan-Islamic group the *Ush-Zhuz*, which joined the Communist Party in 1920; the Crimean Tartar radicals in the *Mili Firqa*; the Persian, pan-Islamist guerrillas in the *Jengelis*, who fought with the Red Army and the Communist Party of Iran; the *Vaisites*, a mystic Sufi brotherhood. The most significant of these alliances was with Enver Pasha, leader of the former Young Turk government, who in 1920 backed the Bolsheviks on the basis of opposition to Western imperialism. His defection to the Basmachi guerrillas in

November 1921 was a serious setback for Moscow's pursuit of nationalist allies.[33]

In those nations where Islam was the dominant religion the equivalents of the Bund and the *Borotbists* were the Muslim Socialist Party, the *Hummet*, and the Persian Communist Party, or *Adelet*, in Azerbaijan. In 1920 these merged with Baku Communists to become the nucleus of the Azeri Communist Party, with a membership of 4,000 and a widespread network of organisation among trade unions, workers' clubs and co-operatives. The first Communist government of Azerbaijan consisted almost entirely of native Azerbaijanis from the left factions of the *Hummet* and *Adelet*.[34]

There was a left shift in Russian Islam after 1917, and by 1920 the Bolsheviks had secured the neutrality or support of most radical national elites in the Muslim East. In Narkomnats, the leadership of the Muslim Commissariat, or Muskom, was largely in the hands of non-Bolshevik Muslims. Smith notes:

> *The Muskom was staffed almost entirely by committed former* ***Jadadists*** [a Muslim intellectual current] *and given real authority, which was backed more often than not by the Bolshevik leadership whenever the Muskom came into conflict with the Narkomnats collegium. As well as the Muskom, Muslims with few Communist credentials were granted leading positions in the departments and sections of Narkomnats for the Kyrgyz, Caucasian Highlanders, Turkestan, Kalmyks, and so on.*[35]

There were strenuous efforts to involve native people in local soviets and party organisations. In those nations where Islam was the main religion, the proportion of party members among locals therefore rose dramatically.[36]

The Bolsheviks also set out to prepare a new generation of national Communists, primarily through the network of party schools and universities: 'European non-Russians received much more training at party schools than Russians... Clearly an intensive effort was made to train communists in Ukraine, Belorussia and Transcaucasia'.[37] The Communist universities also turned out 'significant numbers' of cadres from the Muslim nations. In Moscow in 1921 a majority of places were reserved for entrants from Central Asia.

Out of ten Communist universities in 1924, five were 'national': the Central Asia Communist University (established in 1920); the Communist University of Labourers of the East (1921); the Communist University of Labourers of the National Minorities of the West (1921); the Tartar Communist University (1921); and the Transcaucasian Communist University (1921). By 1924, of 6,073 students attending Communist universities, over half were at these five. This corresponded to the proportion of non-Russians in the population, but it was at a time when 65 percent of party members were Russian. By 1933 Communist universities had been set up in Russia for a whole list of minorities. The training was general and technical, rather than political, and few of the teaching staff were Communists. For example, in Kazan, the capital of the Tartar Autonomous Republic, in 1924 only 19.4 percent were Communists. Smith writes:

> [The universities] *were intended to provide the party with national Communists who had both the technical and literary skills needed to head the national Soviet administrations, the necessary understanding of their own national cultures, and a sufficiently internationalist Communist outlook to ensure a smooth implementation of socialist principles in the national republics. The Bolsheviks made no real attempt to 'Bolshevise' their recruits from the nationalist movements, relying instead on the long term development of a new generation of national Communists.*[38]

Smith gives detailed figures demonstrating the high percentage of natives in national Communist parties by the mid-1920s, especially in leadership positions: 'Although Russians were still over-represented in the Communist Party of the Soviet Union in 1926, their dominance was far less than it had been in 1917'.[39] These national Communist leaders were murdered almost to a man by Stalin in the 1930s.

## Education and language

Education was central to raising the population's cultural level, and the Bolsheviks set out to ensure, where possible, that education of non-Russians took place in the language of their choice. The thinking behind this approach was summed up by a delegate to the First All-Russian Congress on Pre-School Education in the summer of 1919: 'An international spirit is not achieved by lumping together children who cannot understand each other, but rather by introducing in the native tongue the spirit of worldwide revolution'.[40]

In October 1918 Narkomnats published its proposals on schools for national minorities, namely that 25 pupils for each and every age group was sufficient to warrant a native language school. These schools would also study the language of the main local population, although at this stage 'no consideration was given to the possibility of catering for the needs of different national groups within the same school'. Smith finds that numbers of pupils educated in two languages by 1927 were still very small.[41]

But the approach to native language schools was flexible and depended on local factors, such as: the compactness of the national groups or their degree of assimilation, so there were very few native language Ukrainian and Belorussian schools in RSFSR, for example; the political complexion of republican leaderships (eg SR and Bundist influence in Ukraine and Belorussia); and tactical considerations regarding how best to neutralise hardened nationalists by moving them away from more important political and economic structures.

The same policies were adopted in other republics. In Ukraine, after an initial decrease, the number of Ukrainian language schools soared after the appointment of the *Borotbist* Shumskii as Commissar of Education in 1921: 'From hardly any Ukrainian language teachers in 1917, by 1923 there were 45,000 out of the 100,000 deemed necessary, and the printing of Ukrainian language textbooks increased sharply from 1924 onwards'.[42] In 1925 in Armenia 80 percent of elementary school teachers and all those who taught in seven-year or secondary schools were Armenian. In 1923 the Politburo in Moscow authorised 'Muslim spiritual schools', relaxing the separation of church and state in order to encourage Muslim parents to educate their children.[43]

A major problem was the attitude of local officials, typified by Dimanshtein, head of the Jewish Commissariat of Narkomnats and also Russia's chief spokesperson on education, who argued that national schools would undermine proletarian internationalism. Nativisation of higher education was further held back by the dominance of conservative Russians in higher academic posts. The Institute of Oriental Studies, established in Moscow in 1920, was largely an attempt by Narkomnats to combat these attitudes and involve more non-Russians in higher education.[44]

Despite this, and the shortage of finance and teachers, the regime made astonishing strides towards nativising education. By 1927 native language education for national minorities outside their own republic or region was widespread, while in their own republic it was almost total. Smith sums up this achievement: 'Given the scale of the task, the success of the Communists in nativising schools was truly remarkable'.[45]

The result was a massive expansion of learning. According to Hélène Carrère d'Encausse, 'The statistics demonstrate a new ideological reality—the right to education, no longer the privilege of a minority, was a right applied to all, without distinction as to national origin'.[46]

The spread of native language education was impossible, however, without an enormous expansion of printing and publishing in scores of different languages. By 1924, 25 different languages were being published in the Soviet Union, rising to 34 the following year and 44 by 1927. In the Russian Empire many language groups were split into numerous dialects, some close to each other, others more differentiated, and many languages still had no written forms. If children were to be educated in their native languages, then agreement had to be reached on a standard version of a language which might have many dialects.

This choice was often problematic. Such was the case with Uzbek, for example, where initially a rural dialect was preferred as the basis for a standard language, but was later dropped in favour of the dialect of the central urban areas. In general, however, the priority for choosing a dialect was not so much the extent of its spoken use as its role in the literary traditions of written languages, or in the case of previously unwritten languages its suitability for adapting to a written form.[47]

Intimately connected to language was the issue of which alphabet it should be printed in. Russian imperial scholars had adapted the Russian Cyrillic alphabet to the languages of the empire. Many nationalist reformers, with the backing of Muslim religious leaders, sought to restore the Arabic script, while rival reformers believed the Latin alphabet was more democratic and more effective in teaching people to read and write, and that the invention of new scripts based on the Latin would help propel their nations into international economic and cultural discourse. These issues were argued out on a background of fevered debates among rival linguistic schools over the future of language in general—how fast could socialist nations move towards a universal hybrid language? How could languages and scripts be purged of the influence of class society? Both Lenin and Lunacharsky, for example, were in favour of the eventual Latinisation of the Russian language.

Unfortunately Smith's discussion of Bolshevik language and alphabet planning is brief and his conclusions—that these policies were 'idealistic, utopian and even bizarre', and that 'the most practical solution would have been the universal use of Russian'—are hardly supported by the facts.[48] As Michael Smith's excellent *Language and Power in the Creation of the USSR* makes clear, the adoption of a new Latin-based alphabet with no capital letters or punctuation marks by the Yakuts people in Siberia after 1917 was 'a conscious act of national liberation'.[49] The Yakuts were followed during the civil war by several peoples in the North Caucasus, but it was Soviet Azerbaijan that saw the most powerful movement for a Latin script. Azerbaijani Communists spearheaded the movement for Latinisation among Turkic-speaking peoples, leading in the most celebrated case to the successful conversion to a Latin script of Kemal Ataturk's Turkish republic after 1928. Michael Smith remarks on Moscow's 'hands off' approach to policies being pursued in the republics:

> *During these years, amid the civil war and its legacy, the authorities in Moscow were content to leave the matter of alphabet reform to the nationalities themselves. This relative detachment stemmed from their drive to ally*

> *with the 'national progressive intelligentsia' against the 'reactionary clerics' of the established Muslim hierarchy. The Bolsheviks could ill afford to alienate their neo-Arabist allies... Leading Russian Bolsheviks avoided the subject for fear of inciting opposition among devout Muslims.*[50]

It was only later in the 1920s, when Stalinist reaction was in full swing, that Latinisation became a visible public sign of loyalty to the regime. Universal forced Russification began in the early to mid-1930s.[51]

## Theory and practice

Jeremy Smith's dismissive attitude to Bolshevik language policies is symptomatic of his interpretation of Lenin's approach to the national question, the consequences of which surface continually throughout his book. Thus Smith makes a dubious distinction between 'internationalists', who opposed native language education as perpetuating national divisions, and 'nationalists' who were in favour of it. He frequently accuses Lenin and the Bolsheviks of ditching their previous positions and accommodating to nationalism. So Lenin, he states, was originally in favour of Russian becoming the universal language of the former empire, only to switch to support of native language education.[52]

Furthermore, Smith sees almost any concession to national feeling among the minorities as proof that the Bolsheviks were adopting the approach of Austrian Marxists Renner and Bauer, against whom Lenin had polemicised so bitterly and for so long. So according to Smith, the creation of Narkomnats was an Austro-Marxist solution, as was the admission of the *Borotbists* and the Bund into the Ukrainian Communist Party in 1921.[53] Here Smith follows Hélène Carrère d'Encausse, for whom recognising a minority's right to use its own language was 'tantamount to the hitherto rejected idea of extra-territorial cultural autonomy'.[54]

When unable to make the Austro-Marxist label stick, Smith argues that the various solutions to the national question adopted at different points and at different times simply show that Bolshevik national policy was in fact 'based on ambiguous and frequently inconsistent theories', was 'neither foreseen nor planned', 'haphazard and inconsistent', the result of 'on the hoof' and 'ad hoc' decisions. Bolshevik policy on the status of national territories 'was evolving in an improvised manner influenced by several impulses, which included not just Marxist ideology and the beliefs of the Communist Party leadership, but also factors on the ground'.[55]

But this is to miss the point. Marxist doctrine on the national question is *precisely* that policy must take into account specific 'factors on the ground'. Starting from the goal of conscious and voluntary unity of workers of different nations, Lenin arrived at the need for workers in oppressor nations to defend national rights for the oppressed. But he did not elevate 'national rights' to a supra-historical principle—they were subordinate to, and dialectically in harness with, the need for international workers' unity.[56]

To argue that Bolshevik policy was simply haphazard is an unfortunate concession to Pipes, for whom Lenin picked and chose whatever policies he wanted, regardless of principle. For example, Pipes argues that despite his polemics against federalism Lenin was quick to jettison his former rhetoric:

> *Before November 1917 the Bolsheviks, like the Mensheviks, had opposed the federal idea, but now that the state had fallen apart, the pre-revolutionary arguments against this concept were no longer valid. Federalism* [became] *an instrument for welding together the scattered parts of the empire. For this reason...the Bolsheviks reversed their old stand and took over the Socialist Revolutionary programme of a federated Russia.*[57]

On the contrary, it is straightforward to demonstrate that the federation conceived by Lenin was a means and not an end. Transitional in nature, it would enable Russia to await world revolution as a viable state. Federation was a necessary phase on the road to unity and to the transcendence of national differences. Lenin frequently harked back to this basic orientation. 'The federation of nations', he wrote in March 1918, 'is a stage towards a conscious and closer unity of the workers, who will have learned voluntarily to rise above national conflicts.' Subsequently he referred to 'federation as a stage on the way to voluntary fusion'.[58] As Carrère d'Encausse rightly observes, 'Federation was seen [by Lenin] above all as a pedagogical instrument, a school of internationalism'.[59]

In other words, one can only argue that Lenin was inconsistent in his attitude to federalism if one quotes him with no reference to the context in which his arguments were made. Similarly, with regard to native language education, it is a misrepresentation of Lenin's views to cite general remarks about language in a classless, communist future as if they were applicable to a society still in the throes of revolution and civil war.

The Austro-Marxists believed nations were permanent and positive, and that socialism would refine and develop national differences to the maximum. Their views were popular in Russia and threatened to divide the workers' movement by stressing and reinforcing national distinctions.[60] Lenin's pre-revolutionary polemics against them therefore concentrated on the temporary, transitory and historical nature of national culture, and the need for socialists to insist on workers' unity across national divides. But it is quite another matter to suggest that the

Bolsheviks' recognition of the rights of minority peoples to govern issues of education, language and culture was a concession to Austro-Marxism. For example, in 1913 Lenin argued:

> *It would be inexcusable to forget that in advocating centralism we advocate exclusively* ***democratic*** *centralism... Far from precluding local self government, with* ***autonomy*** *for regions having special economic and social conditions, a distinct national composition of the population, and so forth, democratic centralism demands* ***both****... It is beyond all doubt that in order to eliminate all national oppression it is very important to create autonomous areas, however small, with entirely homogeneous populations, towards which members of the respective nationalities scattered all over the country, or even all over the world, could gravitate, and with which they could enter into relations and free associations of every kind.*[61]

Support for autonomous or independent government, creating native leaderships, building up national economies, developing native languages, and strengthening national culture and identity among the non-Russian people of the former empire—these were not 'nationalist' policies, but attempts at concrete application of Lenin's *internationalist* principle that the right to self determination 'implies the maximum of democracy and the minimum of nationalism'.[62] Exactly how this principle was applied depended on a host of factors specific to the peoples in question. The development of capitalism and the general level of culture was often higher in the non-Russian border regions than in the centre, so national movements were stronger. These nations were granted full republican status and maximum independence from Russia—reflected mainly in that they had nominally independent foreign ministries. In other borderlands and within the Russian federation itself, agreements on the extent and limits of autonomy were negotiated with Moscow in the light of the history of different peoples under the empire, the strength of national movements, the size of Communist forces on the ground, the consequences for Bolshevik international policy and for the civil war.

For the first four years of the revolution the last of these was frequently dominant. As Carr puts it, 'The choice was not between dependence and independence, but between dependence on Moscow or dependence on the bourgeois governments of the capitalist world... Everywhere, and in whatever guise the battle was fought, the real issue was the life or death of the revolution'.[63]

It is indisputable that mistakes were made by the Bolsheviks in applying internationalist principles to the non-Russian peoples, and that there were deep divisions within the party on this question—of which more below. But as the above discussion has shown, it is also indisputable that, consistent with their policy of reversing and compensating for Tsarist oppression, the Bolsheviks went to great lengths to protect, nurture and celebrate important aspects of national culture in Russia's former colonies, and that they saw this as a necessary first step towards building trust and strengthening unity between the ex-colonies and the centre. These policies bore fruit in terms of a relative flowering of national culture in the borderlands of the fledgling USSR. As Smith notes, 'While Proletkult and other artistic and historical movements were trying to establish a clear break with the past in Moscow, in the non-Russian regions the trend was towards promoting the nations' historical roots'.[64]

Historians hostile to the Bolsheviks have remarked on the sharp contrast between the brutal Russification of the late 1930s and the national liberalism of the 1920s. This was particularly the case in Ukraine:

> *The 1920s were a time of extraordinary growth, innovation and ferment in Ukrainian culture. Some writers even refer to it as a period of cultural revolution or renaissance.*[65]

Elsewhere, in Kyrgyzia,'the 1920s also saw the beginnings of a truly national literature, based in the first instance on the rich traditions of Kyrgyz epic poetry and the formation of a vernacular standard language'. In Armenia 'Armenian art and culture were promoted, and until the late 1920s the Communists showed caution in their relations with the Armenian church.' In Central Asia in 1922 Moscow introduced wide-reaching reforms: *waqf* lands confiscated by the state were returned to the mosques, religious schools were reopened and *shariat* courts brought back. The Chechen historian Abdurahman Avtorkhanov compares 'the genocide of Stalin and Zhdanov' against the Muslim nations of the Caucasus in the 1940s with the 'most prudent and flexible policy' pursued by the Bolsheviks in the period 1921-1928, which 'was a period of maximum political peace and harmony between the various Caucasian nations and popularity of the Soviet government...everything was done to reinforce the belief of the North Caucasians that they had really achieved their long desired independence.' On Russia's furthest borders, notes Hélène Carrère d'Encausse, 'Russian linguists and ethnologists were instrumental in the creation in 1922 of institutions to protect, rather than destroy or assimilate, the aborigines of the far north and the far east... Soviet policy rejected the alternative of Russification, enabling them to preserve their identities and folklore'.[66]

After the victory of state capitalist counter-revolution under the five-year plans, Stalin did his best to exterminate all memory of national sentiment beneath the weight of a monolithic, bureaucratic Russian culture. The independence of the republics in 1991 and the astonishing resistance in Chechnya are proof that he did not succeed. The disintegration of the USSR should therefore not be seen as the failure of Lenin's national policy—it had been decisively defeated many decades ago.[67] The roots of resistance to Stalinist national oppression were deep, however, and they were strengthened by Lenin and his followers during the brief years of revolution.

## Lenin's last struggle

Within ten years of Lenin's death his legacy of struggle for national liberation lay in ruins. Throughout the latter part of the 1920s the attacks on the non-Russian republics grew more and more strident, and any demand for autonomy in cultural, linguistic or economic spheres came to be branded as a 'nationalist deviation'.

However, it took a few years after the decisive break with the October regime—'the great leap forward' of the first five-year plan and forced industrialisation—for it to be reflected in the reinstatement of Great Russian nationalism as the dominant ideology. Gerhard Simon notes that during these crisis years of the early 1930s Stalin 'managed not to establish another front against the non-Russian peoples. Although political and police actions against prominent national Communists had become more frequent since the late 1920s, the party line on the national issue did not change until 1933—after the conclusion of forced collectivisation'.[68] Between 1930 and 1934 there were even local show trials of workers and officials accused of Russian chauvinism.[69]

When the bloody struggle against the peasantry had been won, however, and workers' solidarity fatally undermined, the bureaucracy found that a Russian nationalism that stressed the continuity between Stalinism and the Tsars was a powerful ideological tool for cementing workers of the main national group—the Russians—to the regime, and for justifying its new, and no less bloody, imperial conquest of the non-Russian republics. The native elites in the non-Russian republics were brutally purged, their scripts were changed back to Cyrillic, and forced Russification took place in schools, culture and all spheres of public life.

One man presided over Bolshevik national policy from 1917 onwards—Joseph Stalin, first as Commissar for the Nationalities from 1917-1923 and then as general secretary of the Communist Party. In perhaps no other field of policy does continuity between Lenin's regime and its successor appear to be so obvious and direct. However, it was also on the national question that Lenin began a sharp attack on Stalin in the last few months of his political life. Moshe Lewin paints a vivid picture of a desperate struggle between the two men, played out over the issues of the status of non-Russian territories within the USSR and the treatment of Communists in Georgia. It reached its climax in the last days before Lenin's third stroke removed him from the scene in March 1923.[70] The Twelfth Party Congress in April that year and the subsequent trial and expulsion from the party of leading Tartar Communist Mir-Said Sultan Galiev in the summer are usually cited as proof that Stalin was victorious and had effected a decisive shift in national policy against the non-Russians.

With access to the archives, in the last two chapters of his book Smith revisits this history. His account is very well written and full of fascinating detail. His evidence that the policies outlined above were not decisively overthrown in 1923 is a useful explanation of the absence of any large-scale purges after the Sultan Galiev affair,[71] and a necessary corrective to those who wish to hurry the story on to the camps, the deliberate famine and the mass national deportations—in 1923 we are still politically a long way from the 1930s.[72]

However, in stressing the elements of continuity in Bolshevik policy in the 1920s, Smith overlooks the danger signs that indicated to Lenin and others that national rights were in peril. Like other recent authors who recognise the relative liberalism of Bolshevik national policy in the 1920s, Smith plays down the extent of disagreement between Lenin and Stalin in 1922-1923. With regard to Lenin's attack on Stalin's plan to make the independent republics part of the Russian Federation, Smith writes, 'The different approaches of Lenin and Stalin were seen to be over matters of detail rather than deep matters of principle... Major principles were not at stake.' Yuri Slezkine too sees the dispute as merely 'another acrimoniously fruitless affair', while Terry Martin concludes, 'One hopes we can finally lay to rest the myth, cultivated by Khrushchev and endorsed by Lewin, that Lenin and Stalin promoted fundamentally different national policies in 1922'.[73]

These conclusions, however, are based on questionable scholarship. Firstly, Smith constantly refers to 'Lenin and Stalin's ideas' as if Stalin shared the same status as a thinker on this issue. But it is wrong to suggest that Lenin and Stalin shared a single common set of ideas on the national question. Stalin's sole theoretical work on the national question was an article written in 1913—this was praised by Lenin on two occasions in that same year, but after that it seems he never mentioned it again.[74] The article's approach to the national question differs fundamentally from Lenin's, ironically borrowing from the Austro-Marxists whom it spends most of its time attacking. For Lenin it was useful to have a non-Russian battering ram in his feud with Renner, Bauer and the Bund, but the article had little significance beyond tactical expedience. Indeed, Stalin's remarks on the national question before 1917 pay only lip service to Lenin's insistence on the right of nations to secede.[75]

Furthermore, in key debates on the national question among Bolsheviks after 1917, Stalin played either a minor role or none whatsoever. His reports on the national question at a party conference in March 1917 and at the Seventh Party Conference in April, where Lenin locked horns with Piatakov and Dzerzhinskii over self determination, argued that national oppression was first and foremost the product of feudalism rather than imperialism. Just five weeks after the October Revolution he narrowed down the population who could have the right to exercise self determination to the workers. When this point was taken up by Bukharin and argued for bitterly against Lenin at the Eighth Party Congress in March 1918, Stalin stayed silent—and later removed the reference to his name from Bukharin's speech when it was published in the journal of Narkomnats.[76]

Within the collegium of Narkomnats Stalin was an isolated figure, unable to win over his closest co-workers. In his articles, reports and negotiations he committed major errors and inconsistencies, and often had to be corrected by Lenin. Until his 1913 article was republished in 1922—almost five years after the revolution—he was unknown outside Russia. Stalin's stubborn, dogged character, his cunning in negotiations, even his ruthlessness, were qualities that Lenin found useful in prosecuting the revolution—but in no sense was Stalin an independent figure in the development and implementation of Bolshevik national policy.[77]

Secondly, one cannot understand the significance of the disagreement between Lenin and Stalin over the national question in 1922-1923 simply by analysing what was written and said at the time—we have to see it within the broad context of the revolution. This is the main weakness of Smith's book, which discusses national policy in almost hermetic isolation from pre-revolutionary society, 1917, the civil war and Stalinist counter-revolution.

The year 1921 found the Bolshevik regime isolated and exhausted by seven years of war. Numerically the working class had shrunk to a small fraction of its former size, barely able to feed itself, while its political leaders lay dead on the battlefields of the civil war. Throughout the state apparatus the Bolsheviks relied on former functionaries of the Tsarist regime, whose influence grew with each new concession to the peasantry and every setback for the world revolution. The Russian nationalists among them raised their heads—anti-Bolshevik émigrés observed the regime's evolution and hoped that Mother Russia was reasserting herself after the chaos of revolution. 'There is no doubt that the infinitesimal percentage of soviet and sovietised workers will drown in that tide of chauvinistic Great Russian riff-raff like a fly in milk,' said Lenin in December 1922.[78]

The Bolsheviks' efforts to combat the rise of Great Russian chauvinism were weakened by deep divisions over the national question within their ranks. While the revolutionary wave was in full flood these disagreements were submerged by the flow of events, but when the ebb set in their significance came to the surface.

The revolution found the party largely unfamiliar with Lenin's arguments on the national question. Speaking during the heated debate on the national question at the Seventh Party Conference in April 1917, the experienced Georgian Bolshevik Filipp Makharadze warned the party not to rush into a decision:

> *The national question is a serious issue, but also a highly complex and confusing one. Unfortunately I have to say that the conference has not had an opportunity to sufficiently clarify this matter... In the way that it has been posed by comrades Lenin and Zinoviev, the question has still not been discussed in the legal press.*

Similarly, in March 1919 the longstanding Russian Marxist Riazanov told the Eighth Party Congress:

> *Our party is completely unprepared to sort out the issue of the right of nations to self determination. I propose we open a discussion on this question in the party and clarify all the disagreements there have been... We have done so little politically that, with a sudden attack on this slogan, we are taking a risk not only on an international scale but also internally within Russia.*[79]

Large numbers of Bolsheviks, including members of the Bolshevik Politburo, central committee and those in leading positions in Narkomnats, reasoned as follows: national oppression is merely one aspect of the oppression of workers by the ruling class; the October Revolution has overthrown the ruling class; therefore there is no need to set up national republics or autonomous territories within Russia; territorial division should be on the basis of economic efficiency; any territorial autonomy is a concession to petty bourgeois nationalism. These comrades made no distinction between the nationalism of the oppressors and that of the oppressed. So the Polish Bolshevik Dzerzhinskii said in April 1917, 'If comrade Lenin accuses Polish comrades of [Russian] chauvinism, then I can accuse him of sharing the same position as Polish, Ukrainian and other chauvinists. I don't know which is better'.[80] State autonomy or independence was nothing but an obstacle to economic centralisation, as the leading Bolshevik Piatakov said in March 1919: 'Given that we are economically uniting...all this notorious self determination is not worth one rotten egg... [We must] stick firmly to the path of strict proletarian centralisation and proletarian unity'.[81] Supporters of this position talked of subordinating the interests of any one nation to those of the world proletariat as a whole, of the stupidity of recognising national rights for the bourgeoisie, and of the impossibility of independence in the epoch of imperialism.

Very early on Lenin recognised that this abstract opposition to national rights could dovetail with Russian chauvinism. 'Scratch a Communist', he said, 'and you'll find a Russian chauvinist.' In Ukraine, for example, in the first two years of the revolution, the results of widespread rejection of Lenin's position by leading Bolsheviks were disastrous.[82]

This was the context in which in 1923 Lenin and Stalin fell out over the national question. Stalin's plan—supported in essence by almost all the republican leaders—to expand the RSFSR to include all the independent republics totally overlooked the danger of Great Russian chauvinism. The crisis in Georgia, where Stalin's henchman Ordzhonikidze had gone so far as to punch a supporter of Georgian independence, shone a bright light on the extent to which Russian chauvinist attitudes had taken root in the state apparatus, assisted by the ultra-left attitudes of many Bolsheviks. The dispute between Lenin and Stalin over the nature of the USSR was therefore no subtle tactical disagreement about whether there should be a little more or a little less centralism in relations between Moscow and the republics. It was about a key political principle. In practice, Stalin's position—whether he realised it or not—was one of centralism on the basis of Russian dominance of the USSR. Lenin's was that of centralism on the basis of democracy, which demanded that Russia did not impose itself on its former colonies.

The key question was this—were concessions to national rights stoking the fires of non-Russian nationalism, or was that nationalism a defensive reaction to Great Russian chauvinism, which was growing ever stronger as reaction set in? In the debates on the national question at the Twelfth Party Congress in March 1923, and again at a meeting of leading party workers from the republics in June, supporters of strict measures to combat 'national deviations' in the republics repeatedly ignored the question of Great Russian chauvinism. Supporters of Lenin, Trotsky and the Georgian Communists, on the other hand, insisted on Russian nationalism as the main threat to Soviet power.[83]

Moreover, the dispute was seen as a matter of fundamental political principle by many of its participants at the time. Lenin said, 'I declare war to the death on Great Russian chauvinism.' In his 'Testament' he talked about a 'campaign of truly Great Russian nationalism', for which Stalin and Dzerzhinskii were responsible, and demanded that Ordzhonikidze be expelled from the party. Trotsky demanded that the Georgians should not be labelled 'deviationists', and told Kamenev, 'On the national question the Stalin resolution is good for nothing. It places the high-handed and insolent oppression by the dominant nation on the same level with the protest and resistance of small, weak and backward nationalities.' The Bulgarian Bolshevik leader Christian Rakovskii said that Stalin's proposals would mark 'a turning point in the entire national policy of our party', comparing them to the New Economic Policy—ie, a major retreat from Communist principles—on the national question. The Georgian 'old Bolshevik' Mdivani warned that 'a certain part of the central committee directly denies the existence of the national question and is entirely infected with [Russian] Great Power tendencies'.[84]

Stalin, on the other hand, accused Lenin of 'national liberalism' and of falling under the influence of 'a couple of Georgian Mensheviks'.[85]

History has proved that Lenin's dire warnings in 1922-1923 were right. A qualitative change was taking place in the party as Stalin and the bureaucracy consolidated their power. Having been a pliable mouthpiece for Lenin's national policies in the early years of the revolution, Stalin became the spokesperson for the bureaucracy as it began to cut itself free from workers' control. The divisions within Bolshevik ranks on the national question helped him to effect a gradual transition from a defender of national rights to the champion of Great Russian chauvinism.

## Conclusion

Lenin's policy on the national question can be summed up as follows. Where it was desired, national populations who had suffered under Tsarism were granted wide-ranging territorial autonomy by Moscow—from local soviets up to and including political independence from Russia at a state level—as far as this was feasible in conditions of foreign intervention and international revolutionary war. Land was confiscated from Russian colonists and returned to native peoples, while refugees displaced by Tsarist deportations, repression and war were given a genuine choice to return to home. The remnants of Russian colonial outposts were politically disenfranchised and, when necessary, repressed.

As a result, these autonomous and independent territories were able to spread their cultural wings and indulge the fullest possible freedom to speak their own languages, write in their own chosen alphabets, worship their own gods and celebrate their own cultural heritage. On the basis of this trust, Moscow endeavoured to strengthen genuine democratic unity between the workers of these nations and Russian workers by building native Communist cadres, spreading education to the masses, raising the proportional and absolute numbers of native workers in urban centres, undermining the power and influence of reactionary religious and political leaders, encouraging native units in the Red Army to wage civil war on their own bourgeoisie, and holding up the ex-colonies freed from oppression by socialist revolution as an example to colonial peoples all over the world.

These polices were implemented to a varying degree and with varying success. They met with obstacles in the form of large-scale foreign intervention on the side of conservative native elites, the residual strength of Russian chauvinism, the weakness of Communist cadres, and divisions in the Bolshevik ranks over national policy. They encountered the greatest difficulties in far-flung areas cut off from Moscow, where Bolsheviks were few in number and lacking in experience. After a few short years Lenin's bold beginnings foundered on the rocks of the revolution's isolation in a backward country and the rise of a chauvinist Stalinist counter-revolution.

Smith's book provides much raw material from which a true picture of a revolutionary national policy emerges—a picture very different from that painted by Cold War historians of the Soviet Union. On the basis of Smith's research we can confidently conclude that tens of millions of non-Russian workers and peasants rallied to the Bolshevik flag not because they were cunningly deceived or saw it merely as the lesser of two evils, but because Bolshevik policy offered real and positive benefits to the victims of racism and colonialism.

The sliver of truth on which anti-Soviet historians feed, however, remains the manner in which Lenin was obliged to subordinate the self determination of nations to the urgent demands of international revolution. By hiding the fact that this was a clear and explicit policy on Lenin's behalf, enemies of Bolshevism claim that Russia's leader jettisoned his principles in favour of imperialist conquest. Any full investigation of Bolshevik policy in this field must therefore examine specific episodes where the Red Army is alleged to have invaded sovereign territory and trampled on national rights—most notably in Ukraine and Georgia. A full refutation of Pipes's book demands case by case treatment of the experience of Sovietisation in different republics.

Any discussion of the Bolsheviks and the national question is incomplete without a comparison of Bolshevik policies with those of the Tsars and Stalinism. The Bolsheviks' achievements stand out in sharp relief on the background of Tsarist despotism, but they can be overlooked altogether if they are not juxtaposed to the full extent of Stalinist reaction. Bolshevik national policy must also be judged in the context of civil war and Lenin's battle for the revolution to spread abroad. The sheer size and diversity of the Soviet Union, however, mean that the records of Bolshevik debates and policy are a rich source of experience on which revolutionaries can draw. They open up a realistic vision of a future for humanity free of national prejudice and division.

**Notes**

I am grateful to Gennady Poberezhni, Ildar Rismukhamedov, Alexander Savchenko and Nicolai Gentchev for comments on the draft. I would welcome further comments at resist_davidcrouch@hotmail.com

1 R Pipes, *The Formation of the Soviet Union: Communism and Nationalism 1917-1923* (Cambridge, Massachusetts, 1997), pv.
2 Ibid, pp280, 276.
3 M Lewin, *Lenin's Last Struggle* (London, 1973).
4 H Carrère d'Encausse, *The Great Challenge: Nationalities and the Bolshevik State, 1917-1930* (New York, 1992), p67. In contrast, Nigel Harris in *National Liberation* (Reno, 1990) devotes just a single sentence to the Bolsheviks' 'genuine efforts to be respectful and protective of national cultures' (p98), and therefore paints a very one-sided and negative picture of Bolshevik national policy. According to Harris, 'The record in practice seemed appalling' and 'hypocritical'—albeit the hypocrisy 'was no more extreme than in other sectors of policy' (pp96, 98). Harris therefore gives a misleading account of Lenin's approach to the national question.
5 H Carrère d'Encausse, op cit, p149.
6 Y Slezkine, 'The USSR as a Communal Apartment, or How a Socialist State Promoted Ethnic Particularism', *Slavic Review* 53:2 (1994), pp414-452; T Martin, 'The Russification of the RSFSR', *Cahiers du Monde Russe* 39:1-2 (1998), pp99-118; T Martin, *The Affirmative Action Empire: Nations and Nationalism in the Soviet Union, 1923-1929* (New York, 2001). In correcting Pipes's account, however, Slezkine in particular disregards the sharp break with the 1920s that took place under Stalin and the systematic national oppression suffered by non-Russian peoples from the mid-1930s.
7 G Simon, *Nationalism and National Policy Towards the Nationalities in the Soviet Union: From Totalitarian Dictatorship to Post-Stalinist Society* (Oxford, 1991), p6.
8 S Blank, *The Sorcerer as Apprentice: Stalin as Commissar of Nationalities, 1917-1924* (Westport, Connecticut, 1994), p285.
9 L Trotsky, *Stalin,* vol 2 (Moscow, 1990), p29.
10 L Trotsky, *The History of the Russian Revolution* (London, 1985), p902.
11 See R Pipes, op cit, pp84, 77, 73.
12 J Smith, *The Bolsheviks and the National Question, 1917-1923* (London, 1999), p29.
13 Ibid, p41.
14 Ibid, pp93-94.
15 R Pipes, op cit, pp89, 86, 93.
16 J Smith, op cit, pp46, 47; R Pipes, op cit, pp181-183. Lenin recommended 'sending to concentration camps all former members of the police, military, security forces, administration etc [in Turkestan] who were products of the Tsarist era and who swarmed around Soviet power because they saw in it the perpetuation of Russian domination.' Quoted in H Carrère d'Encausse, op cit, p96.
17 R Pipes, op cit, p166.
18 J Smith, op cit, p54.
19 Ibid, p51.
20 Ibid, pp54, 55-64.
21 See H Carrère d'Encausse, op cit, for example, and A A Bennigsen and S E Wimbush, *Muslim National Communism in the Soviet Union: A Revolutionary Strategy for the Colonial World* (Chicago, 1980).
22 J Smith, op cit, pp84, 70-78.
23 R Pipes, op cit, p198.

24 J Smith, op cit, p90.
25 Ibid, pp104-105.
26 Ibid, p104; H Carrère d'Encausse, op cit, p198.
27 J Smith, op cit, p133. Characteristically, *korenizatsiia* is mentioned only twice by A A Bennigsen and S E Wimbush, op cit, and even then only in passing.
28 H Carrère d'Encausse, op cit, pp149-150.
29 J Smith, op cit, p113.
30 Ibid, pp113-115. Pipes completely ignores the treatment of Jewish people by the Bolsheviks.
31 R Pipes, op cit, p71.
32 J Smith, op cit, pp116-125.
33 Ibid, pp126-127; R Pipes, op cit, pp256-260.
34 R Pipes, op cit, pp218-220, 229. Smith, unfortunately, has very little to say about the *Hummet*. For a history of the short-lived Bolshevik commune in Baku in 1918, see R Suny, *The Baku Commune, 1917-1918: Class and Nationality in the Russian Revolution* (Princetown, 1972).
35 J Smith, op cit, p131. Note that Smith, in common with most of the literature in this field, often refers to 'Muslim peoples' as a shorthand for peoples in regions where Islam was the dominant religion.
36 Ibid, p132.
37 Ibid, p137.
38 Ibid, pp139-140.
39 Ibid, p140.
40 Quoted ibid, p152.
41 Ibid, pp149, 161. Unfortunately Smith does not elaborate on this point and does not investigate whether Narkomnats' proposals were implemented.
42 Ibid, p155.
43 H Carrère d'Encausse, op cit, p189; J Smith, op cit, p156.
44 J Smith, op cit, pp146, 151-153.
45 Ibid, pp156-157, 145-146. A sense of just how far Stalin went to smash these achievements is given in the memoirs of the Bolshevik linguist Lytkin, who returned from the camps after the Second World War to the Komi republic, where he found that native children were forbidden to speak their native language at school even during playtime—which was the case before 1917. See V Alpatov, *150 Iazykov I Politika, 1917-2000* (Moscow, 2000), pp99-100.
46 H Carrère d'Encausse, op cit, p191.
47 J Smith, op cit, pp162-164.
48 Ibid, pp167, 165.
49 M Smith, *Language and Power in the Creation of the USSR, 1917-1953* (Berlin, 1998), p122.
50 Ibid, p124.
51 It is interesting to note that since 1991 all the ex Soviet republics of Central Asia, plus Tatarstan, Azerbaijan and Moldova, have officially reverted to the Latin script.
52 J Smith, op cit, p162. In a separate article Smith goes further and says that Lenin made 'serious political errors from the point of view of Marxist theory'. See 'The Georgian Affair of 1922: Policy Failure, Personality Clash or Power Struggle?', *Europe-Asia Studies,* May 1998.
53 J Smith, *The Bolsheviks and the National Question*, op cit, pp43, 28.
54 Ibid, p174.
55 Ibid, pp241, 64, 30.
56 See the articles collected in V I Lenin, *Questions of National Policy and Proletarian Internationalism* (Moscow, 1977).
57 J Smith, *The Bolsheviks and the National Question*, op cit, p111.

58 Quoted in H Carrère d'Encausse, op cit, p114.
59 Ibid, p137.
60 C Harman, 'The Return of the National Question', *International Socialism* 56 (Autumn 1992).
61 V I Lenin, op cit, pp38-39, 42. Emphasis in original.
62 Ibid, p84.
63 E H Carr, *The Bolshevik Revolution, 1917-1923*, vol 1 (London, 1966), p273. Trotsky's book on the national question in Georgia, published as *Social Democracy and the Wars of Intervention in Russia, 1918-1921* (London, 1975), reveals the full truth of Carr's words.
64 J Smith, *The Bolsheviks and the National Question*, op cit, p169.
65 O Subtelny, *Ukraine: A History* (Toronto, 1988), p394. It should be noted that Ukraine had hitherto seen some of the worst errors in Bolshevik national policy.
66 S Crisp, 'Kirgiz', in G Smith (ed), *The Nationalities Question in the Soviet Union* (London, 1990), p248; E M Herzig, 'Armenians', ibid, p151; R Pipes, op cit, p259; A Avtorkhanov, 'The Chechens and the Ingush During the Soviet Period and its Antecedents', in M Bennigsen Broxup (ed), *The North Caucasus Barrier: The Russian Advance Towards the Muslim World* (London, 1996), pp192, 155; H Carrère d'Encausse, op cit, pp186-187.
67 Some of the consequences of this defeat for Russian politics today are outlined in 'The Crisis in Russia and the Rise of the Right', *International Socialism* 66 (Spring 1995).
68 J Smith, *The Bolsheviks and the National Question,* op cit, p9. Trotsky makes the same point about the ultra-left 'third period' of Stalinist policy at the time in L Trotsky, *Stalin*, vol 2, op cit, p224. For an interesting discussion of how the Russian leadership groped its way towards Russian chauvinism at this time, see D L Brandenberger, 'The People Need a Tsar: The Emergence of National Bolshevism as Stalinist Ideology, 1931-1941', *Europe-Asia Studies*, July 1998.
69 T Martin, 'The Russification of the RSFSR' op cit, p103.
70 M Lewin, op cit.
71 A fact which mystifies Bennigsen and Wimbush, for example. See A A Bennigsen and S E Wimbush, op cit, p86.
72 Pipes is the obvious example here, although Nigel Harris is also inclined to exaggerate wildly about 1923: 'It was 1914 all over again... The historic position of the Bolshevik Party had thus, without any change of programme, been completely reversed.' N Harris, op cit, pp99, 113.
73 J Smith, op cit, pp188-189; Y Slezkine, op cit, p417; T Martin, review of Jeremy Smith's book in *The Russian Review* 59:1 (January 2000), p143.
74 J Stalin, *Marksizm i Natsional'nyi Vopros* (Moscow, 1949). E van Ree, 'Stalin and the National Question', *Revolutionary Russia* 7:2 (December 1994), pp214-238. Van Ree summarises the extensive research on the history of Stalin's article.
75 E van Ree, op cit.
76 E H Carr, op cit, pp267, 271; L Trotsky, *Stalin*, op cit, p42.
77 See the relevant chapter in Trotsky's *Stalin*, op cit, and pp174, 178, 189.
78 Quoted in T Cliff, *Revolution Besieged: Lenin, 1917-1923* (London, 1987), p409.
79 *Sed'maia (Aprel'skaia) Vserossiiskaia Konferentsiia RSDRP (Bolshevikov): Protokoly* (Moscow, 1958), p224; *Vos'moi S"ezd RKP(b): Protokoly* (Moscow, 1959), p69.
80 *Sed'maia*, op cit, p219.
81 *Vos'moi*, op cit, pp80-81.
82 Ibid, p106. At the Eighth Party Conference in December 1919 Yakovlev talked about how a great mass of chauvinist Russian workers had descended on Ukraine 'like locusts' and behaved like 'conquerors'. Striving to bend the stick to correct the situation, Lenin talked about the need for all Ukrainian Communists to become

*Borotbists*. See *Vos'maia Konferentsiia RKP(b): Protokoly* (Moscow, 1961). Further discussion of the strength of ultra-left views on the national question among Bolsheviks can be found in J D White, 'National Communism and World Revolution', *Europe-Asia Studies* 46:8 (1994), pp1349-1369.

83 *Tainy Natsional'noi Politiki TsK RKP: Stenograficheskii Otchet Sekretnogo IV Soveshchaniia TsK RKP, 1923g* (Moscow, 1992).

84 *Arkhiv Trotskogo: Kommunisticheskaia Oppositsiia v SSSR, 1923-1927* (Moscow, 1990), vol 1, p51; L Trotsky, *My Life* (Harmondsworth, 1985), p506; *Nesostoiavshiisia Iubilei: Pochemu SSSR ne Otprazdnoval svoego 70-Letiia?* (Moscow, 1992), pp118, 123.

85 *Nesostoiavshiisia*, op cit, p114.

**The Socialist Workers Party is one of an international grouping of socialist organisations:**

| | |
|---|---|
| **AUSTRALIA** | International Socialists, PO Box A338, Sydney South |
| **AUSTRIA** | Linkswende, Postfach 87, 1108 Wien |
| **BRITAIN** | Socialist Workers Party, PO Box 82, London E3 3LH |
| **CANADA** | International Socialists, PO Box 339, Station E, Toronto, Ontario M6H 4E3 |
| **CYPRUS** | Ergatiki Demokratia, PO Box 7280, Nicosia |
| **CZECH REPUBLIC** | Socialisticka Solidarita, PO Box 1002, 11121 Praha 1 |
| **DENMARK** | Internationale Socialister, PO Box 5113, 8100 Aarhus C |
| **FINLAND** | Sosialistiliitto, PL 288, 00171 Helsinki |
| **GERMANY** | Linksruck, Postfach 304 183, 20359 Hamburg |
| **GREECE** | Sosialistiko Ergatiko Komma, c/o Workers Solidarity, PO Box 8161, Athens 100 10 |
| **HOLLAND** | Internationale Socialisten, PO Box 92025, 1090AA Amsterdam |
| **IRELAND** | Socialist Workers Party, PO Box 1648, Dublin 8 |
| **NEW ZEALAND** | Socialist Workers Organization, PO Box 13-685, Auckland |
| **NORWAY** | Internasjonale Socialisterr, Postboks 9226 Grønland, 0134 Oslo |
| **POLAND** | Pracownicza Demokracja, PO Box 12, 01-900 Warszawa 118 |
| **SPAIN** | Izquierda Revolucionaria, Apartado 563, 08080 Barcelona |
| **UNITED STATES** | Left Turn, PO Box 445, New York, NY 10159-0445 |
| **ZIMBABWE** | International Socialist Organisation, PO Box 6758, Harare |

**The following issues of *International Socialism* (second series) are available price £3 (including postage) from IS Journal, PO Box 82, London E3 3LH. *International Socialism* 2:58 and 2:65 are available on cassette from the Royal National Institute for the Blind (Peterborough Library Unit). Phone 01733 370 777.**

**International Socialism 2:93 Special issue**
John Rees: Imperialism: globalisation, the state and war ★ Jonathan Neale: The long torment of Afghanistan ★ Anne Alexander: The crisis in the Middle East ★ Mike Gonzalez: The poisoned embrace: Plan Colombia and the expansion of imperial power ★ Chris Harman: The new world recession ★

**International Socialism 2:92 Autumn 2001**
Tom Behan: 'Nothing can be the same again' ★ Boris Kagarlitsky: The road from Genoa ★ Alex Callinicos: Toni Negri in perspective ★ Jack Fuller: The new workerism: the politics of the Italian autonomists ★ Goretti Horgan: How does globalisation affect women? ★ Rumy Hasan: East Asia since the 1997 crisis ★ Charlie Kimber: Dark heart of imperialism ★ Megan Trudell: The pursuit of 'unbounded freedom' ★

**International Socialism 2:91 Summer 2001**
Susan George: What now? ★ Walden Bello: The global conjuncture ★ Chris Nineham: An idea whose time has come ★ Mike Marqusee: Labour's long march to the right ★ Mike Davis: Wild streets—*American Graffiti* versus the Cold War ★ Goretti Horgan: Changing women's lives in Ireland ★ John Lister: We will fight them in the hedgerows ★ Mike Gonzalez: The Zapatistas after the Great March—a postscript ★ Dragan Plavsic: Hoist on their own petards ★

**International Socialism 2:90 Spring 2001**
John Rees: Anti-capitalism, reformism and socialism ★ Chris Harman: Beyond the boom ★ Walden Bello: 2000: the year of global protest ★ Michael Lavalette and others: The woeful record of the House of Blair ★ Brian Manning: History and socialism ★ Peter Morgan: A troublemaker's charter ★

**International Socialism 2:89 Winter 2000**
Lindsey German: Serbia's spring in October ★ Anne Alexander: Powerless in Gaza: the Palestinian Authority and the myth of the 'peace process' ★ Boris Kagarlitsky: The lessons of Prague ★ Mike Gonzalez: The Zapatistas: the challenges of revolution in a new millennium ★ Stuart Hood: Memoirs of the Italian Resistance ★ Esme Choonara: Threads of resistance ★ Megan Trudell: Setting the record straight ★ Judy Cox: Reasons to be cheerful: theories of anti-capitalism ★ Mark O'Brien: A comment on *Tailism and the Dialectic* ★

**International Socialism 2:88 Autumn 2000**
Chris Harman: Anti-capitalism: theory and practice ★ Paul McGarr: Why green is red ★ Boris Kagarlitsky: The suicide of *New Left Review* ★ Gilbert Achcar: The 'historical pessimism' of Perry Anderson ★ Dave Renton: Class consciousness and the origins of Labour ★ Keith Flett: Socialists and the origins of Labour: some other perspectives ★ John Newsinger: Fantasy and revolution: an interview with China Miéville ★

**International Socialism 2:87 Summer 2000**
Lindsey German: How Labour lost its roots ★ Mark O'Brien: Socialists and the origins of Labour ★ Judy Cox: Skinning a live tiger paw by paw ★ Peter Morgan: The morning after the night before... ★ John Newsinger: Plumbing the depths: some recent books on New Labour ★ Abbie Bakan: From Seattle to Washington: the making of a movement ★ Jim Wolfreys: In perspective: Pierre Bourdieu ★ Nick Barrett: Complement to 'Reformism and class polarisation in Europe' ★ Mark Krantz: Humanitarian intentions on the road to hell ★ John Rees: Tony Cliff: theory and practice ★ Ygal Sarneh: A revolutionary life ★ Shaun Doherty: The language of liberation ★

**International Socialism 2:86 Spring 2000**
John Charlton: Talking Seattle ★ Abbie Bakan: After Seattle: the politics of the World Trade Organisation ★ Mark O'Brien: In perspective: Susan George ★ Rob Ferguson: Chechnya: the empire strikes back ★ Lindsey German: The Balkans' imperial problem ★ Megan Trudell: The Russian civil war: a Marxist analysis ★ Robin Blackburn: Reviewing the millennia ★ Jim Wolfreys: In defence of Marxism ★ Judy Cox: Can capitalism be sustained? ★

**International Socialism 2:85 Winter 1999**
Alex Callinicos: Reformism and class polarisation in Europe ★ Michael Lavalette and Gerry Mooney: New Labour, new moralism: the welfare politics and ideology of New Labour under Blair ★ Ken Coates: Benign imperialism versus United Nations ★ John Baxter: Is the UN an alterna-

tive to 'humanitarian imperialism'? ★ John Rose: Jesus: history's most famous missing person ★ Chris Harman: The 20th century: an age of extremes or an age of possibilities? ★ Mike Gonzalez: Is modernism dead? ★ Peter Morgan: The man behind the mask ★ Anne Alexander: All power to the imagination ★ Anna Chen: George Orwell: a literary Trotskyist? ★ Rob Hoveman: History of theory ★ Chris Harman: Comment on Molyneux on art ★

**International Socialism 2:84 Autumn 1999**
Neil Davidson: The trouble with 'ethnicity' ★ Jim Wolfreys: Class struggles in France ★ Phil Marfleet: Nationalism and internationalism ★ Tom Behan: The return of Italian Communism ★ Andy Durgan: Freedom fighters or Comintern army? The International Brigades in Spain ★ John Molyneux: Art, alienation and capitalism: a reply to Chris Nineham ★ Judy Cox: Dreams of equality: the levelling poor of the English Revolution ★

**International Socialism 2:83 Summer 1999**
John Rees: The socialist revolution and the democratic revolution ★ Mike Haynes: Theses on the Balkan War ★ Angus Calder: Into slavery: the rise of imperialism ★ Jim Wolfreys: The physiology of barbarism ★ John Newsinger: Scenes from the class war: Ken Loach and socialist cinema ★

**International Socialism 2:82 Spring 1999**
Lindsey German: The Blair project cracks ★ Dan Atkinson and Larry Elliott: Reflating Keynes: a different view of the crisis ★ Peter Morgan: The new Keynesians: staking a hold in the system? ★ Rob Hoveman: Brenner and crisis: a critique ★ Chris Nineham: Art and alienation: a reply to John Molyneux ★ Paul McGarr: Fascists brought to book ★ Brian Manning: Revisionism revised ★ Neil Davidson: In perspective: Tom Nairn ★

**International Socialism 2:81 Winter 1998**
Alex Callinicos: World capitalism at the abyss ★ Mike Haynes and Pete Glatter: The Russian catastrophe ★ Phil Marfleet: Globalisation and the Third World ★ Lindsey German: In a class of its own ★ Judy Cox: John Reed: reporting on the revolution ★ Kevin Ovenden: The resistible rise of Adolf Hitler ★

**International Socialism 2:80 Autumn 1998**
Clare Fermont: Indonesia: the inferno of revolution ★ Workers' representatives and socialists: Three interviews from Indonesia ★ Chris Bambery: Report from Indonesia ★ Tony Cliff: Revolution and counter-revolution: lessons for Indonesia ★ John Molyneux: The legitimacy of modern art ★ Gary McFarlane: A respectable trade? Slavery and the rise of capitalism ★ Paul McGarr: The French Revolution: Marxism versus capitalism ★ Shaun Doherty: Will the real James Connolly please stand up? ★

**International Socialism 2:79 Summer 1998**
John Rees: The return of Marx? ★ Lindsey German: Reflections on *The Communist Manifesto* ★ Judy Cox: An introduction to Marx's theory of alienation ★ Judith Orr: Making a comeback: the Marxist theory of crisis ★ Megan Trudell: New Labour, old conflicts: the story so far ★ John Molyneux: State of the art ★ Anna Chen: In perspective: Sergei Eisenstein ★ Jonathan Neale: Vietnam veterans ★ Phil Gasper: Bookwatch: Marxism and science ★

**International Socialism 2:78 Spring 1998**
Colin Sparks: The eye of the storm ★ Shin Gyoung-hee: The crisis and the workers' movement in South Korea ★ Rob Hoveman: Financial crises and the real economy ★ Peter Morgan: Class divisions in the gay community ★ Alex Callinicos: The secret of the dialectic ★ John Parrington: It's life, Jim, but not as we know it ★ Judy Cox: Robin Hood: earl, outlaw or rebel? ★ Ian Birchall: The vice-like hold of nationalism? A comment on Megan Trudell's 'Prelude to revolution' ★ William Keach: In perspective: Alexander Cockburn and Christopher Hitchens ★

**International Socialism 2:77 Winter 1997**
Audrey Farrell: Addicted to profit—capitalism and drugs ★ Mike Gonzalez: The resurrections of Che Guevara ★ Sam Ashman: India: imperialism, partition and resistance ★ Henry Maitles: Never again! ★ John Baxter: The return of political science ★ Dave Renton: Past its peak ★

**International Socialism 2:76 Autumn 1997**
Mike Haynes: Was there a parliamentary alternative in 1917? ★ Megan Trudell: Prelude to revolution: class consciousness and the First World War ★ Judy Cox: A light in the darkness ★ Pete Glatter: Victor Serge: writing for the future ★ Gill Hubbard: A guide to action ★ Chris Bambery: Review article: Labour's history of hope and despair ★

**International Socialism 2:75 Summer 1997**
John Rees: The class struggle under New Labour ★ Alex Callinicos: Europe: the mounting crisis ★ Lance Selfa: Mexico after the Zapatista uprising ★ William Keach: Rise like lions? Shelley and the revolutionary left ★ Judy Cox: What state are we really in? ★ John Parrington: In perspective: Valentin Voloshinov ★

**International Socialism 2:73 Winter 1996**
Chris Harman: Globalisation: a critique of a new orthodoxy ★ Chris Bambery: Marxism and sport ★ John Parrington: Computers and consciousness: a reply to Alex Callinicos ★ Joe Faith: Dennett, materialism and empiricism ★ Megan Trudell: Who made the American Revolution? ★ Mark O'Brien: The class conflicts which shaped British history ★ John Newsinger: From class war to Cold War ★ Alex Callinicos: The state in debate ★ Charlie Kimber: Review article: coming to terms with barbarism in Rwanda in Burundi ★

**International Socialism 2:72 Autumn 1996**
Alex Callinicos: Betrayal and discontent: Labour under Blair ★ Sue Cockerill and Colin Sparks: Japan in crisis ★ Richard Levins: When science fails us ★ Ian Birchall: The Babeuf bicentenary: conspiracy or revolutionary party? ★ Brian Manning: A voice for the poor ★ Paul O'Flinn: From the kingdom of necessity to the kingdom of freedom: Morris's *News from Nowhere* ★ Clare Fermont: Bookwatch: Palestine and the Middle East 'peace process' ★

**International Socialism 2:71 Summer 1996**
Chris Harman: The crisis of bourgeois economics ★ Hassan Mahamdallie: William Morris and revolutionary Marxism ★ Alex Callinicos: Darwin, materialism and revolution ★ Chris Nineham: Raymond Williams: revitalising the left? ★ Paul Foot: A passionate prophet of liberation ★ Gill Hubbard: Why has feminism failed women? ★ Lee Sustar: Bookwatch: fighting to unite black and white ★

**International Socialism 2:70 Spring 1996**
Alex Callinicos: South Africa after apartheid ★ Chris Harman: France's hot December ★ Brian Richardson: The making of a revolutionary ★ Gareth Jenkins: Why Lucky Jim turned right—an obituary of Kingsley Amis ★ Mark O'Brien: The bloody birth of capitalism ★ Lee Humber: Studies in revolution ★ Adrian Budd: A new life for Lenin ★ Martin Smith: Bookwatch: the General Strike ★

**International Socialism 2:69 Winter 1995**
Lindsey German: The Balkan war: can there be peace? ★ Duncan Blackie: The left and the Balkan war ★ Nicolai Gentchev: The myth of welfare dependency ★ Judy Cox: Wealth, poverty and class in Britain today ★ Peter Morgan: Trade unions and strikes ★ Julie Waterson: The party at its peak ★ Megan Trudell: Living to some purpose ★ Nick Howard: The rise and fall of socialism in one city ★ Andy Durgan: Bookwatch: Civil war and revolution in Spain ★

**International Socialism 2:68 Autumn 1995**
Ruth Brown: Racism and immigration in Britain ★ John Molyneux: Is Marxism deterministic? ★ Stuart Hood: News from nowhere? ★ Lee Sustar: Communism in the heart of the beast ★ Peter Linebaugh: To the teeth and forehead of our faults ★ George Paizis: Back to the future ★ Phil Marshall: The children of stalinism ★ Paul D'Amato: Bookwatch: 100 years of cinema ★

**International Socialism 2:67 Summer 1995**
Paul Foot: When will the Blair bubble burst? ★ Chris Harman: From Bernstein to Blair—100 years of revisionism ★ Chris Bambery: Was the Second World War a war for democracy? ★ Alex Callinicos: Hope against the Holocaust ★Chris Nineham: Is the media all powerful? ★ Peter Morgan: How the West was won ★ Charlie Hore: Bookwatch: China since Mao ★

**International Socialism 2:66 Spring 1995**
Dave Crouch: The crisis in Russia and the rise of the right ★ Phil Gasper: Cruel and unusual punishment: the politics of crime in the United States ★ Alex Callinicos: Backwards to liberalism ★ John Newsinger: Matewan: film and working class struggle ★ John Rees: The light and the dark ★ Judy Cox: How to make the Tories disappear ★ Charlie Hore: Jazz: a reply to the critics ★ Pat Riordan: Bookwatch: Ireland ★

**International Socialism 2:65 Special issue**
Lindsey German: Frederick Engels: life of a revolutionary ★ John Rees: Engels' Marxism ★ Chris Harman: Engels and the origins of human society ★ Paul McGarr: Engels and natural science ★

**International Socialism 2:63 Summer 1994**
Alex Callinicos: Crisis and class struggle in Europe today ★ Duncan Blackie: The United Nations and the politics of imperialism ★ Brian Manning: The English Revolution and the transition from feudalism to capitalism ★ Lee Sustar: The roots of multi-racial labour unity in the United States ★ Peter Linebaugh: Days of villainy: a reply to two critics ★ Dave Sherry: Trotsky's last, greatest struggle ★ Peter Morgan: Geronimo and the end of the Indian wars ★ Dave Beecham: Ignazio Silone and *Fontamara* ★ Chris Bambery: Bookwatch: understanding fascism ★

**International Socialism 2:62 Spring 1994**
Sharon Smith: Mistaken identity—or can identity politics liberate the oppressed? ★ Iain Ferguson: Containing the crisis—crime and the Tories ★ John Newsinger: Orwell and the Spanish Revolution ★ Chris Harman: Change at the first millenium ★ Adrian Budd: Nation and empire—Labour's foreign policy 1945-51 ★ Gareth Jenkins: Novel questions ★ Judy Cox: Blake's revolution ★ Derek Howl: Bookwatch: the Russian Revolution ★

**International Socialism 2:61 Winter 1994**
Lindsey German: Before the flood? ★ John Molyneux: The 'politically correct' controversy ★ David McNally: E P Thompson—class struggle and historical materialism ★ Charlie Hore: Jazz—a people's music ★ Donny Gluckstein: Revolution and the challenge of labour ★ Charlie Kimber: Bookwatch: the Labour Party in decline ★

**International Socialism 2:59 Summer 1993**
Ann Rogers: Back to the workhouse ★ Kevin Corr and Andy Brown: The labour aristocracy and the roots of reformism ★ Brian Manning: God, Hill and Marx ★ Henry Maitles: Cutting the wire: a criticial appraisal of Primo Levi ★ Hazel Croft: Bookwatch: women and work ★

**International Socialism 2:58 Spring 1993**
Chris Harman: Where is capitalism going? (part one) ★ Ruth Brown and Peter Morgan: Politics and the class struggle today: a roundtable discussion ★ Richard Greeman: The return of Comrade Tulayev: Victor Serge and the tragic vision of Stalinism ★ Norah Carlin: A new English revolution ★ John Charlton: Building a new world ★ Colin Barker: A reply to Dave McNally ★

**International Socialism 2:56 Autumn 1992**
Chris Harman: The Return of the National Question ★ Dave Treece: Why the Earth Summit failed ★ Mike Gonzalez: Can Castro survive? ★ Lee Humber and John Rees: The good old cause—an interview with Christopher Hill ★ Ernest Mandel: The Impasse of Schematic Dogmatism ★

**International Socialism 2:55 Summer 1992**
Alex Callinicos: Race and class ★ Lee Sustar: Racism and class struggle in the American Civil War era ★ Lindsey German and Peter Morgan: Prospects for socialists—an interview with Tony Cliff ★ Robert Service: Did Lenin lead to Stalin? ★ Samuel Farber: In defence of democratic revolutionary socialism ★ David Finkel: Defending 'October' or sectarian dogmatism? ★ Robin Blackburn: Reply to John Rees ★ John Rees: Dedicated followers of fashion ★ Colin Barker: In praise of custom ★ Sheila McGregor: Revolutionary witness ★

**International Socialism 2:51 Summer 1991**
Chris Harman: The state and capitalism today ★ Alex Callinicos: The end of nationalism? ★ Sharon Smith: Feminists for a strong state? ★ Colin Sparks and Sue Cockerill: Goodbye to the Swedish miracle ★ Simon Phillips: The South African Communist Party and the South African working class ★ John Brown: Class conflict and the crisis of feudalism ★

**International Socialism 2:48 Autumn 1990**
Lindsey German: The last days of Thatcher ★ John Rees: The new imperialism ★ Neil Davidson and Donny Gluckstein: Nationalism and the class struggle in Scotland ★ Paul McGarr: Order out of chaos ★

**International Socialism 2:41 Winter 1988**
Polish socialists speak out: Solidarity at the Crossroads ★ Mike Haynes: Nightmares of the market ★ Jack Robertson: Socialists and the unions ★ Andy Strouthous: Are the unions in decline? ★ Richard Bradbury: What is Post-Structuralism? ★ Colin Sparks: George Bernard Shaw ★

**International Socialism 2:18 Winter 1983**
Donny Gluckstein: Workers' councils in Western Europe ★ Jane Ure Smith: The early Communist press in Britain ★ John Newsinger: The Bolivian Revolution ★ Andy Durgan: Largo Caballero and Spanish socialism ★ M Barker and A Beezer: Scarman and the language of racism ★